#2

2/28

Praise for Marvin Meyer
and *Judas:*

"Marvin Meyer's *Judas* leads us into the world of the new Coptic gospel that portrays Judas as the most beloved and insightful disciple of Christ. This book offers a thrilling journey through early Christian texts about Judas, asking the question if the devilish figure of this disciple is founded on historical elements or if it is merely a literary creation. The fluent presentation keeps the reader in suspense from the first to the last page. You won't be able to stop reading this book."

> —Madeleine Scopello, Directeur de Recherche au Centre National de la Recherche Scientifique, Université de Paris IV-Sorbonne, and author of *Femme, Gnose et Manichéisme*

"The earliest New Testament author Paul knew nothing of Judas. But decades later the evangelists created Judas (Yehuda in Hebrew, meaning Jew) as the perfect archetypal betrayer figure for shifting guilt from favored Rome to the Jews for crucifying rabbi Jesus. With Judas as the star villain was born the historical sea of anti-Semitism. The Christians (meaning Messianics), like the Essenes, another early messianic Jewish sect, needed to reject the mother religion in order to bloom as a newly named tree of hope. In his introduction, translation, and sumptuous annotation, the Coptic scholar Marvin Meyer eloquently documents all the ancient legends of Judas. The book's core is the recently found, brilliantly explosive Gnostic *Gospel of Judas,* in which Judas appears as Jesus's most intimate student (disciple). Judas yields his life to free Jesus from bodily bondage and be transfigured in divine light. As Jesus's trusted liberator, the student is not the grotesque demon of the canonical gospels but Saint Judas."

— Willis Barnstone, author of *The Other Bible*

"Marvin Meyer has provided the most convenient collection of all the references to Judas available in early Christian literature."

— James M. Robinson, author of *The Secrets of Judas*

"Marvin Meyer has put together a timely anthology of controversial ancient writings that refer to 'Judas' and 'Judas Iscariot.' He includes canonical texts like the *Gospels of Mark, Matthew, Luke,* and *John,* alongside lesser-known apocryphal texts such as the *Arabic Infancy Gospel* and the *Golden Legend,* and Gnostic gospels like the recently recovered *Gospel of Judas.* Meyer's anthology makes accessible to the general public documents about Judas that are not otherwise readily available."

— April D. DeConick, author of *The Thirteenth Apostle: What the Gospel of Judas Really Says*

"Meyer offers a diverse sampling of interesting and important texts and traditions that relate, or may relate, to the very curious gospel character Judas Iscariot, about whom quite lively debate has been renewed by a recently published ancient manuscript. Meyer's collection and his lucid comments provide general readers with handy access to ancient sources at the heart of the new debates, and an introduction to reasons for some of the controversy."

—Michael A. Williams, Professor of Comparative Religion, University of Washington

"This wide-ranging collection of texts produced from the second to the fifth centuries and beyond clearly shows the interpretive spectrum of the developing Church's struggle with the legendary and controversial figure of the apostle Judas Iscariot."

—John D. Turner, Cotner Professor of Religious Studies, University of Nebraska

"*Judas* is an essential scholarly tool, written in a clear and direct way, for understanding the challenge posed by the recent discovery of the *Gospel of Judas*. This gospel has raised issues regarding the possible reinterpretation of a number of known texts about Judas Iscariot, and many of these texts are presented in this volume and accompanied with helpful commentary."

—Sofía Torallas Tovar, Consejo Superior de Investigaciones Científicas, Madrid, and co-author of *El Evangelio de Judas*

Judas

ALSO BY MARVIN MEYER

The Gnostic Bible

The Gnostic Discoveries

*The Gnostic Gospels of Jesus: The Definitive Collection of Mystical Gospels
and Secret Books About Jesus of Nazareth*

*The Gospels of Mary: The Secret Tradition of Mary Magdalene,
the Companion of Jesus*

Jesus Then and Now: Images of Jesus in History and Christology

The Magical Book of Mary and the Angels

The Nag Hammadi Scriptures

Secret Gospels: Essays on Thomas and the Secret Gospel of Mark

The Secret Teachings of Jesus: Four Gospels

The Unknown Sayings of Jesus

Judas

THE DEFINITIVE COLLECTION OF
GOSPELS AND LEGENDS ABOUT THE
INFAMOUS APOSTLE OF JESUS

MARVIN MEYER

HarperOne
An Imprint of HarperCollins*Publishers*

JUDAS: *The Definitive Collection of Gospels and Legends About the Infamous Apostle of Jesus.*
Copyright © 2007 by Marvin Meyer. All rights reserved. Printed in the United States
of America. No part of this book may be used or reproduced in any manner whatsoever
without written permission except in the case of brief quotations embodied in critical
articles and reviews. For information address HarperCollins Publishers, 10 East 53rd
Street, New York, NY 10022.

HarperCollins books may be purchased for educational, business, or sales promo-
tional use. For information please write: Special Markets Department, HarperCollins
Publishers, 10 East 53rd Street, New York, NY 10022.

HarperCollins Web site: http://www.harpercollins.com

HarperCollins®, ®, and HarperOne™ are
trademarks of HarperCollins Publishers.

FIRST EDITION

Library of Congress Cataloging-in-Publication Data
    Meyer, Marvin W.
        Judas : the definitive collection of gospels and legends about the infamous
    Apostle of Jesus / Marvin Meyer.—1st ed.
        p.   cm.
    Includes bibliographical references.
    ISBN: 978-0-06-134830-3
    ISBN-10: 0-06-134830-9
    1. Judas Iscariot.   2. Gospel of Judas.   I. Title.
    BS2460.J8M49   2007
    226'.092—dc22   2007018365

07 08 09 10 11 RRD (H) 9 8 7 6 5 4 3 2 1

CONTENTS

The Vilification and Redemption of a Disciple of Jesus

THE RECENT PUBLICATION OF THE LONG LOST *GOSPEL OF JUDAS*, with its remarkable portrayal of Judas Iscariot as the disciple closest to Jesus, provides a fitting occasion to reconsider the figure of Judas as presented in ancient texts and traditions.[1] Typically Judas has been demonized in Christian sources as the quintessential traitor, the disciple who betrayed his master for the infamous thirty pieces of silver. The roots of the demonization of Judas go back to the New Testament gospels and the *Acts of the Apostles*, in which the progressive defamation of Judas during the final decades of the first century CE may be traced, and these sorts of themes come to expression in our own day in such popular presentations as *Jesus Christ Superstar*, in which Judas pleads, in song:

I have no thought at all about my own reward.
I really didn't come here of my own accord.
Just don't say I'm damned for all time.

It is instructive to lay out the four gospels of the New Testament in chronological order, from *Mark* through *Matthew* and *Luke* to *John*, in order to read the developing story of Judas as it was written and rewritten in the gospels during the first, formative years. Such a chronological reading makes it clear that, as the decades passed, more and more abuse was heaped upon Judas, and his character was subjected to more and more vilification. In *Mark*, the earliest New Testament gospel, composed around 70 CE, Judas Iscariot hands Jesus over to the authorities, but the motivation of Judas is unclear and the precise nature of his act is uncertain. In *Matthew*, composed a decade or so after *Mark*, Judas is portrayed as an evil man who betrays Jesus for money, and after his heinous act he confesses his guilt and commits suicide by hanging himself—though at least he may be seen as remorseful. In *Luke*, it is said that the devil makes Judas do what he does, and his death in *Acts*, although claimed to take place in fulfillment of prophecy, is depicted as a horrific disembowelment. In *John*, Judas becomes the personification of evil, and Jesus says that Judas is a devil. In *John* 17, the so-called high-priestly prayer, Jesus does not name Judas but refers to him, we may be sure, as "the son of perdition" or "the son bound for destruction." Not only is it announced, in *John* 13, that one of the disciples is unclean and inspired by Satan; Jesus also tells his disciples, in *John* 6, "Didn't I choose you, the Twelve? Yet one of you is a devil."[2]

This process of the demonization of Judas Iscariot continues in Christian literature and art during the decades and centuries that follow. Still, in the writings of Paul, composed before the New Testament gospels, and in some of the early Christian gospels outside the New Testament, no mention whatsoever is made of Judas by name. In *1 Corinthians* 11 Paul does recall, in general, that the night of the last supper was the night Jesus was handed over, but he does not say by whom. Elsewhere Paul proclaims, however, that God was the one who handed Jesus over to be crucified or that Jesus gave himself over to death, and he uses forms of the same Greek verb (*paradidonai*) to describe the act of God or of Jesus as the New Testament gospel authors use to describe the act of Judas. This Greek verb means "give over," "deliver over," or "hand over," and it does not necessarily mean "betray," with all the negative connotations inherent in that word. Paul writes, in *Romans* 8, that God handed over his Son for us all and, in *Galatians* 2, that Jesus as the Son of God loved Paul and handed himself over for Paul.

In other early Christian texts, however, there is an awareness of the New Testament gospel traditions about Judas handing over Jesus, and the legends about Judas grow in number and negativity. Papias, a second-century Christian author who wrote *Expositions of the Sayings of the Lord*, calls Judas an unbeliever and betrayer who would never see the kingdom of God, and Papias depicts the appearance of Judas in life and in death in disgusting detail. He writes that Judas becomes so bloated that he cannot get through passageways, he cannot see through his swollen eyelids, and when he relieves himself, he produces pus and worms. Tormented in life,

Judas kills himself, and the land where he is buried develops a sickening stench from his putrid body. In one manuscript of the *Gospel of Nicodemus* (or the *Acts of Pilate*), a colorful detail is added to the traditional tale in the *Gospel of Matthew* about Judas committing suicide. Judas, it is said, is hunting for a rope with which he can hang himself, and he asks his wife, who is roasting a chicken, to help him. She responds by saying that Judas has nothing to fear from the crucified Jesus he has betrayed, since Jesus cannot rise from the dead any more than the roasting chicken can speak, whereupon the chicken on the spit spreads its wings and crows—and Judas goes out and hangs himself.

The *Arabic Infancy Gospel* includes a story suggesting that Judas was possessed by Satan even as a child. According to this text, little Judas goes out to play with Jesus, and Satan makes him want to bite Jesus. When he is unable to do so, he hits Jesus instead on his right side, Jesus ends up crying, and Satan races off as a mad dog. The spot where Judas struck Jesus, the text declares, is the very spot where "the Jews" would pierce the side of Jesus during his crucifixion. The reference to the piercing of the side of Jesus is from the *Gospel of John*, but there it is a Roman soldier who pierces Jesus's side. By the time of the *Arabic Infancy Gospel*, perhaps in the fifth or sixth century, "the Jews" are being blamed for all that has to do with the crucifixion and death of Jesus, the Christian Savior and Son of God, and Judas is understood to be, in youth and adulthood, an evil Jew.

Other portrayals of Judas in Christian literature show a similar interest in depicting him as a Jew who is the embodiment of evil. In one text Judas is described as having infiltrated the Jesus movement in order to catch Jesus saying or doing something for which he could be condemned. Judas's wife is sometimes said to be complicitous in the plot to hand Jesus over, and as a result a baby boy of Joseph of Arimathea, who is being cared for by Judas's wife, refuses to nurse with her. Elsewhere it is suggested that Judas ends up worshiping the devil, and in the *Golden Legend* he is depicted as a Christian Oedipus who kills his father (Reuben [Ruben] or Simon[3]) and marries his mother (Ciborea). Judas finally is subjected to punishments and torments in hell, and Jesus says to him, in a text with anti-Semitic proclivities, "Tell me, Judas, what did you [gain] by handing me, [your Master], over to the Jewish dogs?"[4]

The interpretation of Judas Iscariot as the evil Jew who betrayed Jesus has contributed a great deal to the history and development of anti-Semitic thought. Judas becomes a building block in the construction of the hateful system of anti-Semitism, and Judas himself appears, in legend and artwork, as a caricature of a wicked and greedy Jew who turns against his friend for money. Until the discovery and publication of the *Gospel of Judas*, this Judas, the quintessential traitor, provided the dominant image of Judas Iscariot in Christian discussions.

Codex Tchacos

The *Gospel of Judas* was discovered in the 1970s, in Middle Egypt, in the region of al-Minya, although the precise circumstances of the discovery remain unknown. The *Gospel of Judas* is one text among others in an ancient codex, or book, now called Codex Tchacos. According to Herbert Krosney, who has pieced together much of the story of the ancient gospel and the bound book, Codex Tchacos was found by local fellahin, or farmers, in a cave that was located at the Jabal Qarara and had been used for a Coptic burial. The cave contained, among other things, Roman glassware in baskets or papyrus or straw wrappings. Krosney writes, in *The Lost Gospel:*

> The burial cave was located across the river from Maghagha, not far from the village of Qarara in what is known as Middle Egypt. The fellahin stumbled upon the cave hidden down in the rocks. Climbing down to it, they found the skeleton of a wealthy man in a shroud. Other human remains, probably members of the dead man's family, were with him in the cave. His precious books were beside him, encased in a white limestone box.[5]

What happened to the *Gospel of Judas* and Codex Tchacos thereafter is not a pretty matter. The gospel and the codex apparently were displayed, stolen, and recovered; eventually the codex was taken to Europe, where it was shown to scholars for possible purchase. The purchase price proved to be beyond the financial reach of any of the parties viewing the texts, and the owner left without a sale. Later the *Gospel of Judas* and the other texts turned up in the United States, and for sixteen years the papyrus was locked away in a safe-deposit box in Hicksville, New York, on Long Island. A safe-deposit box is not the ideal place to store fragile papyrus. In the humidity of Long Island, with nothing resembling a climatized environment, the papyrus began to disintegrate. A potential American buyer obtained the texts for a time, and in a misguided effort to separate the papyrus pages he put the papyrus in a freezer, thereby causing additional damage. He also had problems with cash flow, so that he was forced to surrender some of his claims to ownership of the texts. In short, on account of human greed and ineptitude, the lost *Gospel of Judas* was in danger of being lost once again.[6]

By the time the Maecenas Foundation and the National Geographic Society were able to secure the codex for conservation and scholarly examination, the papyrus was in wretched shape. In 2001 the prominent Swiss papyrologist Rodolphe Kasser saw the codex, and he says he let out a cry of shock and surprise. What was once a papyrus book was now a mass of fragments thrown into a box. He began to work with another expert, Florence Darbre, at conserving the papyrus and placing fragments together. After years of painstaking work nothing short of a papyrological miracle occurred. The box of a thousand fragments became a book once again, with a legible Coptic copy of the *Gospel of Judas*.[7]

The work of reconstruction is based on the features of ancient papyrus sheets, which were formed by placing strips of the papyrus reed at right angles—horizontal and vertical strips. The individual fibers of papyrus often have anomalies, for example, darker strands or unusual characteristics, that can be traced from one fragment to another and allow separate fragments to be connected. These factors, along with observations on the profile of the edges of fragments and the sequence of letters and words on the fragments, contribute to the work of assembling fragments. The entire operation may be compared to working on a jigsaw puzzle, except that in this case 20–25 percent of the pieces are missing and the edges of the pieces are rough and uneven. Nonetheless, fragment may be connected to fragment until whole pages and texts are restored.

When the large and small papyrus fragments of the *Gospel of Judas* and the other texts in the collection were assembled, the result was a codex. Codex Tchacos is one of the earliest examples of a bound book, and this codex should add a great deal to our knowledge of the history of bookbinding. Many of the procedures employed in the construction of an ancient book like Codex Tchacos continue to be used, more or less, to the present day. In the ancient world, several papyrus sheets were cut to size and folded in half to form quires, and the quires were bound into leather covers made from the skin of sheep or goats. In order to transform the resultant softback into a hardback book, cartonnage, or scrap papyrus from the wastebasket (letters, receipts, and the like), was pasted into the cover of the codex. The cartonnage from the cover of Codex Tchacos may well provide dates and indications of places that could contribute to accurate information about the production of Codex Tchacos.

Yet we do have a general idea of when Codex Tchacos was assembled, and we are confident that the codex is an authentic ancient manuscript. I know of no papyrus that has been as thoroughly tested as the papyrus of Codex Tchacos. It has been subjected to carbon-14 dating tests, and although Florence Darbre admits that it nearly broke her heart to destroy even tiny portions of the codex in order to test its antiquity, the carbon-14 tests have yielded results that date the codex to 280 CE, plus or minus sixty years. Further, an ink test—called a TEM, or transmission electron microscopy test—confirms the same range of dates for the ink. And the paleography, or handwriting style, and the religious and philosophical contents of the codex place it comfortably in the period at the end of the third or beginning of the fourth century.[8]

Codex Tchacos, copied near the beginning of the fourth century, contains several texts, including the *Gospel of Judas*, preserved in Coptic or late Egyptian translation. As currently known, there are some sixty-six pages in the codex. The *Gospel of Judas*, like the other texts in the collection, was almost certainly composed in Greek sometime before the late third or early fourth century—probably quite a bit before—and subsequently translated into Coptic and copied onto the pages of the codex. The other texts in Codex Tchacos are (1) a copy of the *Letter of Peter to Philip*, also known from the Nag Hammadi library, which was discovered in the 1940s in Egypt; (2) a text entitled *James*, a copy of a document referred to as the *First Revelation of James* and also known from the Nag Hammadi library; and (3) after the *Gospel of Judas*, a fragmentary text, previously unknown, provisionally entitled the *Book of Allogenes*, or *Book of the Stranger*, in which Jesus is depicted as a stranger in this world. There may have been additional texts in the codex, and Gregor Wurst, who collaborated on the publication of the *Gospel of Judas* and Codex Tchacos, has discovered a fragment with what appears to be a page number—108—that could extend the length of the codex far beyond sixty-six pages. Further, fragments with references to Hermes Trismegistus, the hero of Hermetic spirituality, have been identified by Jean-Pierre Mahé, so that Codex Tchacos may well have included a Hermetic text—perhaps a Coptic translation of *Corpus Hermeticum XIII*. But then where is the rest of Codex Tchacos? Has it disintegrated into dust? Or is it in the hands of collectors and others somewhere in the world?[9]

The Gospel of Judas

Doubtless the most significant text in Codex Tchacos is the *Gospel of Judas*.[10] The *Gospel of Judas*, so named in the manuscript itself, gives a presentation of the good news of Jesus with a mystical, Gnostic emphasis. The term "Gnostic" comes from the Greek word *gnôsis*, which means "knowledge"—specifically mystical knowledge and spiritual insight. According to the *Gospel of Judas* and other Gnostic gospels, the true mystery of human life is that we have a spark of the divine within us, a bit of the spirit of God in our hearts, but so often we do not know it because of ignorance and distractions in our lives. Salvation for Gnostics, then, means knowing ourselves, coming to a knowledge of our inner selves as the divine within, so that we may experience bliss. Obviously this sort of spirituality has much in common with forms of Hinduism, Buddhism, and other religions that have spread throughout the world.[11]

Hence, the *Gospel of Judas* proclaims a way of salvation through wisdom, knowledge, and enlightenment. The gospel highlights the figure of Judas Iscariot, who is acclaimed in the *Gospel of Judas* as the disciple closest to Jesus who understands Jesus completely and does all that Jesus asks of him. The gospel includes features that reflect Jewish and Greco-Roman—and particularly Platonic— themes, and in the end Jesus approaches his death, with his friend Judas, in a way that is somewhat reminiscent of Socrates in the *Phaedo*. For Jesus, as for Socrates, death is not to be faced with fear, but is to be anticipated with joy, as the soul or inner person is to be freed from the body of flesh.

The *Gospel of Judas* opens with an announcement of the revelatory encounters Jesus is said to have had with the disciples and especially Judas near the end of his life: "The secret revelatory discourse that Jesus spoke with Judas Iscariot in the course of a week, three days before his passion."[12] After this opening of the gospel, Jesus approaches his disciples as they are gathered for a holy meal, and he laughs. Jesus laughs a great deal in the *Gospel of Judas*, particularly, it seems, because of the foibles and absurdities of human life. Here the disciples protest against his laughter, but Jesus says that he is not laughing at them at all, but at the way they take their religious rituals (in this instance, the holy meal) so seriously, as if their God demands such observance. Jesus invites the disciples to stand before him and face him, but none of them can do it, except Judas, who stands before Jesus but averts his eyes in modesty. Then Judas offers his confession of who Jesus is—the true confession, according to the *Gospel of Judas*. He says to Jesus, "I know who you are and from what place you have come. You have come from the immortal realm of Barbelo, and I am not worthy to pronounce the name of the one who has sent you."[13] To state that Jesus is from the immortal realm of Barbelo is to profess that Jesus comes from the divine and is a child of God, and the name Barbelo, most likely derived from Hebrew, means something very much like "God in Four"—that is, God as known through the tetragrammaton, the holy name of God in Jewish tradition, YHWH (Yahweh).

In the central portion of the *Gospel of Judas*, Jesus takes Judas aside and explains to him the fundamental issue in human life as Gnostic mystics conceive of it: how does the light and spirit of God come from the transcendent realm of the divine into our hearts and lives? Jesus reveals this mystery to Judas by describing the descent or devolution of the divine light into this world below from the infinite realm of God above. Jesus begins by saying to Judas, "[Come], that I may teach you about the things . . . [that] no person will see. For there is a great and infinite realm, whose dimensions no angelic generation could see, [in] which is the great invisible [Spirit], which no eye of angel has seen, no thought of the mind has grasped, nor was it called by a name."[14] In a manner reminiscent of Jewish mysticism—such as we see in Jewish Kabbalah, with its tree of life and its Sefirot, or channels of divine energy emanating from Ein Sof, the infinite God—Jesus tells Judas, and the readers of the *Gospel of Judas,* that from the transcendent world of the divine there flow forth first one who is self-conceived, and then angels, messengers, attendants, aeons, luminaries, heavens, firmaments, and even an ideal image of Adamas, or Adam the first man, down to this world. This world of ours, however, with its limitations, hardships, mortality, and darkness, comes from the creative work of lower angelic beings with names appropriate for their ignorant involvement in the material world: Nebro, meaning "rebel"; Yaldabaoth, meaning "child of chaos"; and Sakla, meaning "fool"—names from the Aramaic language. In related Gnostic texts the demiurge is also named Samael, Aramaic for "blind god." In the stark contrast between the light and knowledge of God and this world of darkness and ignorance lies the human dilemma for Jesus, Judas, and all of us: the light and spirit of God have come down into our hearts, but we are still trapped within an imperfect world and bodies of flesh that prevent us from realizing our true divine destiny. We need liberation.

Near the conclusion of the *Gospel of Judas,* after Jesus has explained everything, he turns to Judas and says, "You will exceed all of them (probably the other disciples). For you will sacrifice the man who bears me."[15] In saying this, Jesus is announcing that Judas will turn him (or his body) over to the authorities to be crucified, and so, it is implied, Jesus will be freed of the body of flesh that hinders the true spiritual person within. Judas himself is transfigured and realizes his enlightened state—unless it is Jesus who is transfigured and leaves his body behind[16]—and Judas proceeds to do what Jesus has indicated: he turns him in to the authorities. Thus, I suggest, Judas shows that he is the best friend and most faithful disciple of Jesus in the *Gospel of Judas*. Judas Iscariot, a disciple of Jesus who was vilified and marginalized in much of Christian tradition, is rehabilitated and redeemed in the *Gospel of Judas*.

Judas Reconsidered

We can be assured that historians, theologians, and other scholars will be studying the *Gospel of Judas* for decades to come in order to analyze its place in the history of early Christianity. The present Coptic translation of the *Gospel of Judas* was prepared, as we have noted, around 300 CE, but the original *Gospel of Judas* must have been composed in Greek in the middle part of the second century, only a few decades after the New Testament gospels were written.[17] With its mystical message and its sympathetic portrayal of Judas Iscariot, the *Gospel of Judas* will help scholars rewrite much of the history of the church during the early period.

For scholars and others, the *Gospel of Judas* raises important issues for reflection and evaluation. To begin with, the *Gospel of Judas* underscores the fact that the early church was a very diverse phenomenon, with different gospels, different understandings of the good news, and different ways of believing in Jesus and following him. Frequently it has been suggested, initially in the New Testament *Acts of the Apostles* and more definitively by the church historian Eusebius of Caesarea, that the Christian church developed

as a unified movement with a singular view of truth and orthodoxy and a common commitment to the eradication of falsehood
and heresy.[18] The *Gospel of Judas*, with its startling presentation of
Jesus and Judas, reminds us that the story of the church, from
its earliest days, discloses a variety of manifestations of Christian
thought. From the beginning, the church has been characterized
by diversity, and that rich heritage of diversity continues to the
present day.

The *Gospel of Judas* raises the issue of the nature of orthodoxy
and heresy in an especially vivid way. The *Gospel of Judas* was referred to by its title around 180 CE in the writings of the heresy
hunter Irenaeus of Lyon, who maintained that this gospel was
a pernicious piece of heresy. The *Gospel of Judas*, in turn, throws
accusations back in the face of the leaders and members of the
emerging orthodox church.[19] This argument about who is right
and who is wrong—that is, who is orthodox and who is hereti-
cal—is not only about theology and doctrine. It is a dispute with
rhetorical and political overtones, and the winner in the debate is
determined by who has the most convincing arguments, the most
powerful voices, and the most votes as decisions are made in the
life of the church. So, from a historical perspective, we may con-
clude that when Irenaeus and friends, who represent the thought
of the emerging orthodox church and consider themselves to be
thoroughly orthodox, speak of what is orthodox and what is he-
retical among the options in the early church, they are not just
identifying orthodoxy and heresy. They are creating the categories
orthodoxy and heresy.[20]

With its provocative picture of a rehabilitated Judas Iscariot,
no longer the traitor but now the friend of Jesus, the *Gospel of Judas*

raises questions about the image of Judas Iscariot in the New Testament gospels.[21] The positive place of Judas in the *Gospel of Judas* may remind us of the hints about the positive character of Judas in the New Testament gospels, in spite of their eventual demonization of him. In the New Testament gospels, Judas is chosen by Jesus to be a part of the inner circle of disciples—the Twelve, in anticipation of a new Israel, with its twelve tribes—and according to the *Gospel of John*, Judas was entrusted with the care of the group's finances. If Judas is said to be the one dipping his bread into the sauce with Jesus at the last supper, does that mean he was understood to be sitting next to Jesus, perhaps as one of his closest friends? If Judas kissed Jesus in the garden, in a greeting between friends still practiced throughout the Middle East today, does that intimate that there were close ties between Judas and Jesus? What did Jesus have in mind when he told Judas to do what he had to do, and do it quickly?

William Klassen, author of *Judas: Betrayer or Friend of Jesus?* and a proponent of a more positive way of looking at Judas, wonders whether there might have been some agreement between Jesus and Judas—recall that the verb ordinarily employed to describe the act of Judas, *paradidonai*, does not necessarily mean "betray." Maybe Judas agreed to introduce Jesus to the proper authorities in Jerusalem so that Jesus could present his vision of the kingdom and help to prevent an outbreak of violence. And perhaps something went terribly wrong. No wonder Judas may have felt so bad about the way things turned out.[22]

In his book—written before the *Gospel of Judas* was available—Klassen outlines five conclusions about the act of Judas that emerge from his reading of the New Testament texts. (1) Judas seems to have gotten together with the high priest and those with him in order to arrange a meeting with Jesus. (2) All the parties in the discussion, Klassen theorizes, wished to avoid hostility and violence. (3) Judas may have appealed to the policy of Jesus himself in such issues of discussion and potential disagreement, that the best recourse is direct encounter with the issues and the people representing the issues. Klassen adds:

> If Judas was indeed a disciple concerned about financial matters, he would have been sensitive to the financial needs of the Temple in a way that Jesus might not have been. He may have thought that, by meeting Temple authorities, Jesus could become better disposed toward the traditional way in which changes were made in the Temple and that Caiaphas could get a better understanding of the reform program Jesus had in mind for the renewal of Israel.

(4) In acting in this manner, Judas would have been following accepted Jewish practice, and he was doing the right thing by letting the high priest know what Jesus was teaching, especially about the Temple. (5) Thus, Judas may have announced to the high priest and his colleagues that Jesus was willing to meet with them, particularly in the light of his premonitions of death. Klassen states, "Having been told by Jesus to do what he had to do quickly, Judas could have assured the high priests that Jesus would not offer resistance, nor would he encourage his followers to resist his arrest."[23]

Klassen closes his analysis with an evaluation of what Judas may have done as a friend of Jesus:

> What precisely was Judas's contribution? I submit that in the grand scheme of things, it was quite modest. In discussions with Jesus, he had often heard

Jesus criticize the Temple hierarchy. When Judas reminded Jesus that his own advice had always been to rebuke the sinner directly, Jesus may have said that an occasion to confront the high priest directly had not appeared. Perhaps at that point Judas offered to arrange it, hoping that the process of rebuke would work. At the same time, he may have questioned Jesus about his own faithfulness to his mission. All of this could have led to a plan whereby Judas would arrange a meeting with Jesus and the high priests, each agreeing to that meeting on their own terms and with their own hopes for the outcome. This role of the "handing over" was later transformed into a more sinister one, especially after Judas had died at his own hand. Whether the reader is able to accept this interpretation of the earliest traditions available to us, I submit that it is at least as plausible as the very negative view of Judas that still pervades the church but rests on a very shaky foundation.[24]

An early Christian text outside the New Testament, the *Dialogue of the Savior* from the Nag Hammadi library, provides more information about a disciple named Judas who was close to Jesus, but precisely who this Judas is remains unclear. The *Dialogue of the Savior* presents Jesus in conversation with his disciples on various topics, some of which are familiar from other texts, including Gnostic texts like the *Gospel of Judas*. Three disciples are singled out by name: Matthew (one of the men known by that name), Mary (most likely Mary Magdalene), and Judas. Because of the similarities of portions of the *Dialogue of the Savior* and sayings from the *Gospel of Thomas*, it may be supposed (as I have argued elsewhere) that the *Dialogue of the Savior* is dependent upon sayings traditions in the *Gospel of Thomas* and that the disciple Judas who is in dialogue with Jesus in the *Dialogue of the Savior* is Judas Thomas, Judas "the Twin," who sometimes is claimed, most notably in the world of Syrian Christianity, to be the twin brother of Jesus. In the *Gospel of Thomas* it is maintained that Judas Thomas recorded the hidden or secret sayings of his brother Jesus. Now, however, especially after the discovery and publication of the *Gospel of Judas,* it may be proposed that the disciple Judas in the *Dialogue of the Savior* is Judas Iscariot, incorporated into the text as one of the disciples most intimate with Jesus and in deep discussion with Jesus about the most profound questions of the universe. Such is also the place of Judas Iscariot in the *Gospel of Judas,* where Jesus reveals the mysteries of the world to him.[25]

In the *Dialogue of the Savior,* Judas raises questions and offers observations about the nature of the cosmos and the life of the followers of Jesus, and he is taken up, with Matthew and Mary, to experience a vision of the consummation of heaven and earth that may recall the transfiguration scene in the *Gospel of Judas.* At one point in the text, Judas asks, "Tell [us], Master, what [existed] before [heaven and] earth came into being?"[26] A little later Judas himself observes, "Look, [I] see that all things are [just] like signs over [the earth], and that is why they have come to be in this way."[27] Jesus provides a revelatory response to the questions of Judas and the others, and, the text states, Judas reacts with piety and devotion: "When Judas heard this, he bowed down, fell on his knees, and praised the Master."[28]

Thus, the *Gospel of Judas* may provide the occasion for the reexamination of the figure of Judas Iscariot in the New Testament and other early Christian literature, with a fuller recognition of his positive character. Could this be the time for the much maligned disciple to be restored at the side of Jesus once again, as St. Judas?

Historical or Literary Figure?

The figure of Judas Iscariot remains elusive. How to evaluate sources that relate to traditions of Judas—especially the extent to which they may apply to a historical person named Judas or be literary creations—is open for discussion and debate. The singer Bob Dylan puts it well in his song "With God on Our Side":

> *In many a dark hour*
> *I've been thinkin' about this,*
> *that Jesus Christ*
> *was betrayed by a kiss.*
>
> *But I can't think for you,*
> *you'll have to decide*
> *whether Judas Iscariot*
> *had God on his side.*

After the discovery of the *Gospel of Judas* and the reexamination of other early sources that deal with Judas, it may be thought that Judas Iscariot had God on his side—before he was forced to submit to the poison pens of editors and interpreters who were eager to cast him as a betrayer of Jesus and an altogether evil man. That many of those editors and interpreters were driven by motives shaped by the desire to blame the Jewish people and an evil Jewish man for what happened to Jesus on the cross seems evident. But what can we say about the historical person of Judas?

To begin with, we may reiterate that in early versions of the New Testament gospel tradition and the *Gospel of Judas,* Judas seems to have been understood to be a close disciple of Jesus, and these more affirmative assessments may apply to a historical Jewish disciple in the Jesus movement. As we have noted, Paul, the earliest New Testament author, knows nothing of a betrayal of Jesus by a renegade disciple named Judas, even though he does refer to the Twelve. In the New Testament stories of the arrest and crucifixion of Jesus, much of the power and poignancy of the account of Judas handing Jesus over to the authorities is linked to the hints of his positive character. According to the New Testament gospels, Jesus is handed over by one of his dearest friends. The fact that the New Testament gospel authors concede that Judas was part of the inner circle of the Twelve, in spite of their accusations against him, and the somewhat convoluted way in which the *Acts of the Apostles* eventually finds a way to replace Judas with Matthias in the apostolic group may suggest that Judas Iscariot as a saintly figure could be based in history.

But we may be able to pursue the argument about the historical or nonhistorical character of Judas further. It may be concluded that the person of Judas Iscariot—including the figure of the wicked betrayer—is partially or entirely a fictional character. To many ancient readers of gospels as well as some modern readers, the name Judas—Yehuda in Hebrew, taken to mean "praised"—sounds like "Jew," so that the New Testament accounts may wish to proclaim that "the Jew" turned Jesus in. The meaning of "Iscariot" is debated by scholars. Some propose that it means "man of Kerioth" or "man of the city"; others understand it as a nickname for one of the Sicarii, the Jewish assassins opposing Roman occupation by force; and still others suggest different etymologies. "Iscariot" as "man of Kerioth" may be the best interpretation of the meaning of the name we can come up with.[29]

In addition, it should be noted that the New Testament gospel narratives of the passion of Christ are created largely from citations out of the Jewish Scriptures, particularly the *Psalms*, and elements in the story of Judas and his act of handing Jesus over reflect passages in the Jewish Scriptures (for example, on Judas kissing Jesus and then turning him in, compare Joab preparing to kiss and then killing Amasa in 2 *Samuel* 20; on Judas receiving thirty pieces of silver, compare the price for the shepherd king in *Zechariah* 11; on bad people like Judas dying badly, compare the accounts of the deaths of Eglon, Sisera, Korah, Dathan, and Abiram, Absalom, Ahithophel, and Amasa). Furthermore, the story of Joseph being sold for twenty pieces of silver to a band of traders heading for Egypt, in *Genesis* 37, may also be compared with the account of Judas and Jesus, and it is particularly interesting to note that the brother of Joseph who comes up with the idea of selling Joseph is Judah, or Judas, as he is named in the Septuagint. *Psalm* 41 may bring to mind the episode of Judas eating with Jesus and then handing him over. In this psalm the Hebrew poet complains, "Even my close friend, whom I trusted, who ate of my bread, lifted up his heel against me."[30]

Similar betrayal stories are known from world literature, and Dennis MacDonald has advanced the controversial but fascinating theory that Mark and other early Christian authors (such as the other New Testament gospel authors who follow Mark) are fundamentally dependent upon Homer for their presentations of Judas and other characters in the gospel stories.[31] MacDonald believes that early Christian writers, particularly Mark, adopted and adapted themes from the great Greek epic poet in interpreting Jesus in the image of Achilles. This theory, derived from the literary concept of *mimêsis,* or "imitation," is made possible by the suggestion that authors like Mark, who wrote in Greek, acquired their knowledge of and facility with the Greek language in school by reading and reflecting upon Homer.

In his evaluation of the story of Judas, MacDonald refers to Melanthius, the treacherous goatherd who, near the end of the *Odyssey,* offers his support to the suitors vying for the love of Penelope by betraying Odysseus and bringing armor and weapons from the storeroom for the suitors who are opposed to Odysseus. For his despicable deeds, Melanthius is killed and his body is mutilated. His hands, feet, nose, and ears are cut off, and his genitals are fed to the dogs. According to MacDonald's theory, *Mark* and the other gospels portray Judas as a traitor like Melanthius, and in their accounts Judas is made to betray Jesus in imitation of Melanthius betraying Odysseus.

Although we do well to be cautious about MacDonald's theory, with its Homeric preoccupations, his argument is thoughtful and smart, and it highlights the prevalence of betrayal stories in ancient literature. To this extent I am in agreement with MacDonald: the evidence of such betrayal stories in the broader world of ancient literature—including the Jewish Scriptures—may lead to the conclusion that Judas the betrayer may be taken more as a literary than a historical figure.[32]

Whether we decide that Judas Iscariot is a first-century disciple of Jesus or a fictional character in the gospel accounts, Judas may now emerge as a much more positive figure in early Christian literature. With this collection of Judas texts, readers can examine the literary materials and, in the spirit of Bob Dylan, decide for themselves who Judas was. In any case, after the *Gospel of Judas* and the reexamination of New Testament and other early Christian sources, it may be difficult to maintain that Judas was simply the evil betrayer of Jesus. Rather, in these accounts a more attractive and inspiring Judas comes forward, within the story of Jesus's life and death, as a model of what it means to be a disciple of the Master.

Finally, as I reflect upon Judas texts ancient and modern, especially the *Gospel of Judas,* I am reminded of what Nikos Kazantzakis has to say about Judas in *The Last Temptation of Christ.* Although Kazantzakis has his own interests in Jesus and Judas, his portrayal of a conversation between the two may function as an invitation to examine the place of Judas in the *Gospel of Judas* and the other texts in a fresh and creative manner:

> *"Judas,"* Jesus answered after a deep silence, *"I am now going to confide a terrible secret to you."*
>
> *Judas bowed his red-haired head and waited with gaping mouth.*
>
> *"You are the strongest of all the companions. Only you, I think, will be able to bear it. I have said nothing to the others, nor will I. They have no endurance."*
>
> *Judas blushed with pleasure. "Thank you for trusting me, Rabbi," he said. "Speak. You'll see: I won't make you ashamed of me."*
>
> *"Judas, do you know why I left my beloved Galilee and came to Jerusalem?"*
>
> *"Yes," Judas answered. "Because it is here that what is bound to happen must happen."*
>
> *"That's right; the Lord's flames will start from here."* [33]

In Kazantzakis, and in many of the texts presented here, the story of Judas and Jesus is filled with an abundance of flames, and the flames, I trust, may produce not only fire and heat, but also light.

About This Book

In this book, I present a selection of texts that deal with the figure of Judas Iscariot, including New Testament texts, the *Gospel of
Judas*, and other early and later Christian literature. The New Testament texts in Chapter 1 represent the earliest testimonies about
Judas, and relevant passages from Paul, the synoptic gospels of
Mark, Matthew, and *Luke*, the *Gospel of John*, and the *Acts of the Apostles*
are given in the order of the New Testament narrative plot. The
centerpiece of the book is Chapter 2, the *Gospel of Judas*, with its
stunning new vision of Judas and Jesus. In Chapters 3, 4, and 5
are given translations of three other Gnostic texts—the *Dialogue
of the Savior*, the *Concept of Our Great Power*, and the "Round Dance
of the Cross"—which may contribute to our knowledge of Judas
traditions. Chapter 6 presents a series of additional texts on Judas,
some from what are today rather obscure sources, and these texts
provide glimpses of the vilification of Judas and the emergence of
anti-Semitic themes through the centuries. In Chapter 7, the account of Joseph in *Genesis*, passages from the book of *Psalms*, and
lines from the great Greek poet Homer offer evidence of traitors
before Judas—Judah, or Judas, and the other brothers of Joseph,
the duplicitous friend of the poet in *Psalm 41*, and Melanthius the
goatherd in the *Odyssey*. The book concludes with a bibliography
of works on Judas Iscariot and the traditions relating to him.

Most of the texts presented here are my translations. The selec-
tions from Sedulius's *Paschal Hymn* have been translated by Patrick
McBrine of the University of Toronto, and the selections from the
Golden Legend and Homer's *Odyssey* have been translated by Jonathan
Meyer of Yale University. Several of the translations—of the

Gospel of Judas, the *Dialogue of the Savior,* the *Concept of Our Great Power,* and the "Round Dance of the Cross"—have been prepared for other volumes published by HarperOne (*The Gnostic Gospels of Jesus* and *The Nag Hammadi Scriptures*). Within the translations, square brackets indicate textual restorations, and pointed brackets indicate textual emendations. Ellipsis dots indicate lacunae, or gaps in the text; three dots are used for lacunae of a line or less of text and six dots for lacunae of more than a line. Notes are added in order to clarify difficult passages and refer to important parallels.

CHAPTER ONE

Judas in the New Testament

THAT JESUS OF NAZARETH WAS HANDED OVER TO BE CRUCI-fied toward the end of his short but eventful life is proclaimed by Paul and the authors of all the New Testament gospels, but with a variety of emphases. They also offer differing assessments of who actually handed Jesus over, and, if Judas Iscariot is thought to have done so, what the precise role of Judas might have been. Paul of Tarsus is the earliest author represented in the New Testament; he penned his letters to churches around the middle of the first century CE. The New Testament gospels were written some time thereafter: *Mark* was composed around the year 70 CE and the gospels of *Matthew* and *Luke* a decade or two after *Mark*. It is generally assumed that the gospels of *Matthew* and *Luke* made use of a version of the *Gospel of Mark* as one of their literary sources along with the *Sayings Gospel Q,* a text that contained a series of sayings of Jesus with limited narrative. The *Gospel of John* was written about

90 CE, and although it differs considerably from the gospels of *Mark, Matthew,* and *Luke,* all four gospels share a central interest in the story of the crucifixion of Jesus and its significance, and all four gospels place the figure of Judas Iscariot in the middle of that story.

Paul proclaims in his letters that Jesus was handed over or delivered over to his death by crucifixion, but he never mentions Judas Iscariot in connection with the handing over of Jesus. In fact, he never mentions Judas Iscariot at all. The Greek term used by Paul to describe the act of handing Jesus over to be crucified is *paradidonai,* the same verb employed in the New Testament gospels for the act of Judas. Traditionally that Greek verb has been translated as the English verb "betray" when used in connection with the act of Judas, but the Greek verb typically has a much more neutral—or even positive—meaning than the word "betray" connotes. Paul uses that very verb, *paradidonai,* in the context of the preaching of the gospel to the people of Corinth when he writes, "I received from the Lord what I also handed over (*paredôka*) to you" (*1 Corinthians* 11:23; cf. also 15:3). In the same verse in *1 Corinthians* 11, when Paul discusses the content of his proclamation, he declares that Jesus shared the last supper with his disciples "on the night when he was handed over," and he makes use of the same Greek verb (*paredideto*). In this passage Paul observes that Jesus was handed over, but he does not indicate who did the handing over or what the act of handing over entailed. Elsewhere in his letters, Paul clarifies who, in his opinion, was responsible for handing Jesus over to be crucified: either Jesus handed himself over (*Galatians* 2:19–20) or God handed Jesus over (*Romans* 8:31–32).

In any case, there is no explicit thought in the letters of Paul that Judas Iscariot handed over or betrayed Jesus. When Paul refers to the Twelve in *1 Corinthians* 15:5, he does so with no qualification and with no suggestion that one of the Twelve, Judas, may have been out of the circle of the Twelve or replaced by another (Matthias) to restore the number of the Twelve. If the risen Christ, according to Paul, appeared to the Twelve after the resurrection, does that mean that Paul presumes that none of the Twelve—not even Judas—was missing at the time of the appearance?

In the New Testament gospels, however, the authors are convinced that Judas Iscariot (the son of Simon Iscariot, according to the *Gospel of John*) was one of the Twelve, the inner circle of followers around Jesus, and that Judas himself was involved in handing Jesus over to the authorities. The specification of twelve men who constitute a special cadre of disciples or apostles is based on the belief that the church is a new Israel, with twelve apostolic founders comparable to the twelve sons of Jacob and twelve tribes of Israel. In my opinion, it is unlikely that this concept goes back to the historical Jesus and the men and women gathered around the historical Jesus. I believe it is much more likely that there were both men and women in the inner circle of supporters with Jesus, and whether there were ten, twelve, fourteen, or twenty such disciples at a given time remains uncertain. The New Testament gospel authors and other early Christian writers after them are convinced that there were twelve and that they were all male—though they are not as certain about exactly which men constitute the Twelve. Nonetheless, the New Testament gospel authors all include Judas Iscariot in the list, but the mention of Judas the son of James in the list in *Luke* (6:16) and *Acts* (1:13) and the omission of Thaddeus (or Lebbaeus) leaves two disciples named Judas among the Twelve.

As noted above, the authors who composed the New Testament gospel accounts are unanimous in their claims that Judas Iscariot is the one who handed Jesus over or, as becomes more emphatic with the passage of time and the increase in hostility against Judas and Jewish people, the one who betrayed Jesus. Still, a careful reading of the New Testament accounts makes it clear, in spite of the beginning of the demonization of Judas already apparent in the New Testament gospels—especially the later gospels—that there seem to be subtle suggestions that Judas may have been a good Jew and a valued disciple of Jesus who was devoted to his master and close to him. If he handed Jesus over to the authorities, what was the intent? William Klassen's perspective may be instructive in this regard. In the conclusion to *Judas: Betrayer or Friend of Jesus?* he writes:

> The early sources do tell us that Judas "handed Jesus over" to the high priest, but that act came as no surprise to Jesus. Indeed, it is never described by him in any of the sources as a betrayal. When words like treason, intrigue, deceit, greed, avarice, disillusionment, villainy, failure, and iniquity are used to describe the actions or person of Judas, we look in vain for New Testament texts for support. Above all, the relations between Judas and Jesus seem to have been warm and friendly.[1]

And as for the death of Judas, the two different New Testament accounts in *Matthew* 27:3–10 and *Acts* 1:3–26—death by hanging and death by disembowelment—are dramatically different from one another yet equally reminiscent of traditional death stories, so that it is difficult to draw any historical conclusions regarding how Judas may have died. Further, according to the *Gospel of Judas* (44–45), Judas envisions himself dying in yet a third way, by being stoned to death by the other disciples.

In the end, Judas Iscariot, as presented in the New Testament gospels, is a fascinating character. The story of Judas told in the

New Testament is, in a sense, a tale for the ages—a person is given over to his eventual fate by a dear friend. So it also was with Joseph the son of Jacob in *Genesis*, with the Hebrew poet and his trusted companion in *Psalm* 41, with Odysseus and his friend Melanthius in Homer's *Odyssey*, and with others. So it may be with many of us in our own experience. It is no wonder that theologians, authors, and artists have turned to Judas with great interest and have portrayed him often as a reprehensible traitor and occasionally as a close friend of Jesus. The more positive image of Judas, which is presented quite forcefully in the *Gospel of Judas*, may already be hinted at in the accounts of Judas in the New Testament gospels.

Jesus and the Gospel Are Handed Over, According to Paul

1 Corinthians 11:23–24

(23) For I received from the Lord what I also handed over[2] to you, that the Lord Jesus, on the night when he was handed over,[3] took bread, (24) and after giving thanks, he broke it and said, "This is my body, which is for you. Do this in my memory."[4]

Galatians 2:19–20

(19) For through the law I have died to the law, so that I might live for God. (20) I have been crucified with Christ. No longer do I live, but Christ lives in me. The life I live in the flesh I live by faith in the Son of God, who loved me and handed himself over[5] for me.

Romans 8:31–32

(31) So what shall we say about this? If God is for us, who is against us? (32) He (God) who did not spare his own Son, but

handed him over[6] for all of us—won't he also, along with him, graciously give us all things?

Judas as One of the Twelve

1 Corinthians 15:3–5

(3) For I handed over[7] to you among the first things[8] what I also received, that Christ died for our sins, in accordance with the scriptures, (4) that he was buried, that he was raised on the third day, in accordance with the scriptures, (5) and that he appeared to Cephas,[9] and then to the Twelve.[10]

Mark 3:13–19

(13) He (Jesus) went up on the mountain[11] and called to him those he wished, and they came to him. (14) And he appointed twelve[12] that they might be with him and he might send them out to preach (15) and have authority to cast out demons: (16) Simon, to whom he also gave the name Peter, (17) and James the son of Zebedee and John the brother of James, to whom he also gave the name Boanerges,[13] which means Sons of Thunder, (18) and Andrew and Philip and Bartholomew and Matthew and Thomas and James the son of Alphaeus and Thaddeus[14] and Simon the Cananaean[15] (19) and Judas Iscariot, who finally handed him over.

Matthew 10:2–4

(2) First, Simon, called Peter, and Andrew his brother, and James the son of Zebedee, and John his brother, (3) Philip and Bartholomew, Thomas and Matthew the tax collector, James the son of Alphaeus,

and Thaddeus,[16] (4) Simon the Cananaean,[17] and Judas Iscariot, the one who finally handed him over.[18]

Luke 6:14–16

(14) Simon, whom he named Peter, and Andrew his brother, and James and John, and Philip and Bartholomew (15) and Matthew and Thomas, and James the son of Alphaeus, and Simon who was called the Zealot, (16) and Judas the son of James,[19] and Judas Iscariot,[20] who became a traitor.[21]

Judas Said to Be a Devil

John 6:64–71

(64) (Jesus:) "There are some of you who do not believe." For Jesus knew from the first who of them were not believers and who would hand him over. (65) And he would say, "This is why I told you that no one can come to me unless the Father has granted it to him."

(66) From then on many of his disciples turned back and would no longer travel with him.

(67) So Jesus said to the Twelve, "You do not also want to leave, do you?"

(68) Simon Peter answered him, "Master,[22] to whom shall we go? You have the words of eternal life, (69) and we have come to believe and know that you are the Holy One of God."

(70) Jesus answered them, "Didn't I choose you, the Twelve? Yet one of you is a devil." (71) He was referring to Judas, the son of Simon Iscariot, for he, one of the Twelve, was going to hand him over.

Judas Objects to Perfume Being Wasted

John 12:1–8

(1) Six days before Passover, Jesus came to Bethany, where Lazarus lived, whom Jesus had raised from the dead. (2) There they prepared a dinner in his honor; Martha did the serving, and Lazarus was one of those reclining at the table with him. (3) Mary took about a pint[23] of expensive perfume of pure nard and anointed Jesus's feet and wiped his feet with her hair. And the house was filled with the fragrance of the perfume.

(4) But one of his disciples, Judas Iscariot, who was going to hand him over, said, (5) "Why wasn't the perfume sold for three hundred denarii[24] and the money given to the poor?" (6) Now, he said this not because he cared about the poor but because he was a thief, and as the keeper of the money bag, he would help himself to the money that was put into it.

(7) Then Jesus said, "Leave her alone. Let her keep it for the day of my burial. (8) For you will always have the poor among you, but you will not always have me."

Some (or the Disciples) Object to the Anointing at Bethany

Mark 14:3–9

(3) While he (Jesus) was in Bethany, reclining at the table in the home of Simon the leper, a woman came in with an alabaster jar of very expensive perfume of pure nard, and she broke the jar and poured the perfume on his head.

(4) Some,[25] however, were displeased and said to themselves, "Why has this perfume been wasted? (5) For she could have sold

this perfume for more than three hundred denarii[26] and given the money to the poor." And they scolded her.[27]

(6) But Jesus said, "Leave her alone. Why are you bothering her? She has done a lovely thing to me. (7) For you will always have the poor among you, and whenever you want you can do something good for them, but you will not always have me. (8) She has done what she could. She has anointed my body ahead of time for my burial. (9) I tell you the truth,[28] wherever the gospel is preached in all the world, what she has done will also be told in memory of her."

Judas Plans to Hand Jesus Over

Mark 14:10–11

(10) And Judas Iscariot, one of the Twelve, went off to the high priests to hand him over to them. (11) When they heard, they were delighted, and they promised to pay him in silver.[29] And he began to look for a way to hand him over at the right time.

Matthew 26:14–16

(14) Then one of the Twelve, named Judas Iscariot, went to the high priests (15) and said, "What are you willing to pay me if I hand him over to you?" They offered him thirty silver coins.[30] (16) And from that moment he began to look for the right time to hand him over.

Luke 22:3–6

(3) Now, Satan entered into Judas, called Iscariot, who was of the number of the Twelve. (4) He went off to discuss with the high

priests and officers how he might hand him over to them. (5) They were delighted, and they agreed to pay him in silver.³¹ (6) He accepted the offer, and he began to look for the right time to hand him over to them, when no crowd was around.

Jesus Washes the Feet of the Disciples, Most Likely Including Judas

John 13:1–20

(1) Before the Passover festival, Jesus knew that his hour had come to leave this world and return to the Father. Having loved his own who were in the world, he loved them to the end.

(2) Dinner was being served, and the devil had already planted it in the heart of Judas, the son of Simon Iscariot, to hand him over. (3) Jesus knew that the Father had put all things into his hands, and that he had come from God and was going back to God. (4) So he got up from dinner, took off his outer garment and set it aside, and wrapped a towel around himself. (5) Then he poured water into a basin, and he began to wash the feet of the disciples and dry them off with the towel that was wrapped around him.³²

(6) He came to Simon Peter.

He said to him, "Master, are you going to wash my feet?"

(7) Jesus answered and said to him, "At this moment you do not know what I am doing, but later you will understand."

(8) Peter said to him, "No, you will never wash my feet."

Jesus answered, "Unless I wash you, you have no part with me."

(9) Simon Peter said, "Then, Master, not only my feet, but also my hands and my head."

(10) Jesus said to him, "Someone who has bathed needs only to wash the feet; the body is clean all over. And you are clean—but

not all of you." (11) For he knew who was going to hand him over. That is why he said, "Not all of you are clean."

(12) When he had washed their feet, he got dressed and returned to his place. He said to them, "Do you understand what I have done for you? (13) You call me Teacher and Master, and what you say is right, for that is what I am. (14) So if I, your Master and Teacher, have washed your feet, you also ought to wash each other's feet. (15) I have set you an example: you should do as I have done for you. (16) I tell you the truth,[33] a servant is not greater than his master, nor is a messenger greater than the one who sent him. (17) If you know these things, blessed are you if you do them.

(18) "I am not speaking about all of you. I know the ones I have chosen. But the scripture is to be fulfilled: 'The one who eats of my bread has lifted up his heel against me.'[34] (19) I am telling you this now, before it happens, so that when it does happen, you will believe that I am. (20) I tell you the truth,[35] whoever accepts one that I send accepts me, and whoever accepts me accepts the one who sent me."

Judas Participates in the Last Supper

Mark 14:17–21

(17) When it was evening, he (Jesus) came with the Twelve. (18) And as they reclined at the table and were eating, Jesus said, "I tell you the truth,[36] one of you who is eating with me will hand me over."[37]

(19) They began to be upset and to say to him, one after another, "It isn't me, is it?"

(20) He said to them, "It is one of the Twelve, the one who is dipping into the bowl with me. (21) For the Son of Humanity[38] is

departing, as it is written of him, but woe to that person by whom the Son of Humanity is handed over. It would have been better for that person if he had not been born."[39]

Matthew 26:20–25

(20) When it was evening, he was reclining at the table with the Twelve. (21) And as they were eating, he said, "I tell you the truth,[40] one of you will hand me over."[41]

(22) They became very upset, and each of them began to say to him, in turn, "It isn't me, is it, Master?"

(23) He answered and said, "The one who dips his hand in the bowl with me—this is the one who will hand me over. (24) The Son of Humanity is departing, as it is written of him, but woe to that person by whom the Son of Humanity is handed over. It would have been better for that person if he had not been born."

(25) Judas, who was to hand him over, answered and said, "It isn't me, is it, Rabbi?"

He said to him, "You said it."

Luke 22:14, 21–23

(14) When the hour arrived, he took his place at the table, and the apostles were with him. . . .

(21) (Jesus:) "But look, the hand of the one who is going to hand me over is with me on the table.[42] (22) For the Son of Humanity is leaving, as it has been decreed, but woe to that person by whom he is handed over."

(23) And they began to question among themselves which of them it might be who would do such a thing.

John 13:21–30

(21) After he said these things, Jesus became troubled in spirit, and he spoke up and said, "I tell you the truth,[43] one of you will hand me over."

(22) The disciples looked around at each other; they were at a loss concerning which one he meant. (23) One of them, the disciple Jesus loved,[44] was reclining close to Jesus. (24) Simon Peter motioned to that disciple and said to him, "Tell us who it is he is referring to."

(25) Thus, leaning back on Jesus, he said to him, "Master, who is it?"

(26) Jesus answered, "It is the one to whom I shall give this piece of bread after I dip it." Then he dipped the piece of bread and took it and gave it to Judas, the son of Simon Iscariot. (27) As soon as he gave Judas the bread, Satan entered into him.[45]

Then Jesus said to him, "What you are going to do, do quickly." (28) Now, no one at the table knew why he said this to him. (29) Some thought that since Judas was the keeper of the money bag, Jesus was telling him, "Buy whatever we need for the festival," or to give something to the poor. (30) So when he had taken the bread, he left at once. It was night.

Judas as the Only Lost Disciple

John 17:11–12

(11) (Jesus:) "I am no longer in the world, but they are still in the world, and I am coming to you.[46] Holy Father, protect them through your name that you have given me, that they may be one

even as we are one. (12) When I was with them, I protected them and kept them safe through your name that you have given me. Not one of them has been lost, except the son of perdition,[47] in order that the scripture might be fulfilled."

Judas Hands Jesus Over to the Authorities

Mark 14:43–46

(43) Immediately, while he (Jesus) was still speaking, Judas, one of the Twelve, came around. With him was a crowd armed with swords and clubs, from the high priests, scholars, and elders.[48]

(44) Now, the one who was to hand him over had arranged that a signal be given to them, saying, "The person I shall greet with a kiss is he. Take him into custody and lead him away safely."

(45) Immediately he arrived, approached him, and said, "Rabbi," and he kissed him. (46) And they laid their hands on him and held him fast.[49]

Matthew 26:47–50

(47) While he was still speaking, look, Judas, one of the Twelve, came by. With him was a great crowd armed with swords and clubs, from the high priests and elders of the people.

(48) Now, the one who was to hand him over had arranged that a signal be given to them, saying, "The person I shall greet with a kiss is he. Take him into custody."

(49) Immediately he approached Jesus and said, "Hello, Rabbi," and he kissed him.

(50) And Jesus said to him, "My friend, why have you come here?"[50]

Then they came and laid their hands on Jesus and held him fast.[51]

Luke 22:47–49

(47) While he was still speaking, look, a crowd came near, with the man called Judas, one of the Twelve, leading them. He walked up to Jesus in order to give him a kiss.

(48) And Jesus said to him, "Judas, are you handing over the Son of Humanity with a kiss?"[52]

(49) When those around him saw what was about to happen, they said, "Master, should we strike with our swords?"

John 18:1–9

(1) When he had said these things, Jesus went out with his disciples across the Kidron Valley. There was a garden there, and he and his disciples visited it.

(2) Now, Judas, who was about to hand him over, also knew of this place, because Jesus often went there with his disciples. (3) So Judas came there, bringing with him a detachment of soldiers and officers from the high priests and Pharisees, with their lamps and torches and weapons.

(4) Jesus, knowing everything that was going to happen to him, went out, and he said to them, "Whom are you looking for?"

(5) They answered him, "Jesus the Nazarene."[53]

He said to them, "I am he." Judas, who was handing him over, was standing there with them. (6) But when he said to them, "I am he," they backed off and fell to the ground.

(7) Once again he asked them, "Whom are you looking for?"
They said, "Jesus the Nazarene."

(8) Jesus answered, "I told you, I am he. So if you are looking for me, let these go." (9) This was so that the word he had spoken would be fulfilled: "I have not lost one of those you have given to me."[54]

Judas Repents and Dies by Hanging

Matthew 27:3–10

(3) When Judas, who had handed him over, saw that he (Jesus) had been condemned, he was filled with regret, and he returned the thirty silver coins[55] to the high priests and elders, (4) saying, "I have sinned by handing over a man of innocent blood."

But they said, "What is that to us? That's your business."[56]

(5) He threw the silver into the Temple and left,[57] and he went off and hanged himself.[58]

(6) The high priests gathered the coins and said, "It would not be right to put this money into the Temple treasury, since it is blood money."

(7) So they came up with a plan, and they used the money to buy the Potter's Field as a burial ground for foreigners. (8) Consequently, that field is called the Field of Blood to the present day.[59] (9) Then what was spoken by Jeremiah the prophet was fulfilled: "And they took the thirty silver coins, the price set for a person—which is the price set among the people of Israel—(10) and they gave the money for the Potter's Field, as the Lord commanded me."[60]

Judas Falls to His Death, and Matthias Replaces Him in the Twelve

Acts 1:13–26

(13) When they (the disciples) arrived,[61] they went upstairs to the room where they were staying: Peter and John and James and Andrew, Philip and Thomas, Bartholomew and Matthew, James the son of Alphaeus and Simon the Zealot, and Judas the son of

James.[62] (14) They all with one mind joined together in prayer, along with the women and Mary the mother of Jesus and his brothers.

(15) In those days Peter stood up among the brothers and sisters—a group of about one hundred twenty in all—and he said, (16) "Brothers and sisters,[63] it was necessary that the scripture be fulfilled which the holy Spirit proclaimed beforehand through the mouth of David concerning Judas, who became a guide for those who arrested Jesus. (17) For he was one of our number, and he shared in this ministry. (18) Now, from the compensation for his wrongdoing this man bought a piece of land,[64] and there he fell face first, and his body burst open and all his intestines spilled out.[65] (19) This became known to everyone living in Jerusalem, so that field was called in their language Akeldama—that is, Field of Blood.[66] (20) For it is written in the book of Psalms:

Let his habitation become desolate,
and let there be none to dwell in it.[67]

Again:

Let another assume his position as overseer.[68]

(21) "So, one of the men who have accompanied us during the entire time that the Master Jesus went in and went out among us, (22) beginning from the baptism of John until the day when he was taken up from us, must become a witness with us of his resurrection."

(23) They proposed two, Joseph called Barsabbas, who was also called Justus, and Matthias. (24) And they prayed and said, "Lord, you who know everyone's heart, show us which one of these two

you have chosen (25) to assume the place of this ministry and position of an apostle, which Judas abandoned to go to his own place."

(26) They cast lots, and the lot fell to Matthias. And he was added to the eleven apostles.

CHAPTER TWO

The Gospel of Judas

THE *GOSPEL OF JUDAS*, FOUND AS THE THIRD TEXT WITHIN Codex Tchacos, is preserved in the form of a Coptic translation of a Greek gospel that was originally composed sometime around the middle of the second century CE. In his tract *Against Heresies* (1.31.1), written around 180, Irenaeus of Lyon denounced the *Gospel of Judas* as a wicked work fabricated by Gnostics; Pseudo-Tertullian, Epiphanius of Salamis, and a number of other heresiologists also had similarly unkind words to say about the *Gospel of Judas*. According to Irenaeus, Gnostics claimed that Judas Iscariot was acquainted with the ways of the true God, Judas alone of the disciples knew the truth, and as a result he performed the mystery of the betrayal, or the handing over, of Jesus—which is linked to the dissolution of all things earthly and heavenly. Irenaeus intimates that these sorts of Gnostic ideas are included in the *Gospel of Judas,* and his brief description fits quite well the present Coptic text entitled the *Gospel of Judas.*

The *Gospel of Judas* in Codex Tchacos is given its title at the conclusion of the text. The Coptic title (based on the Greek) is *peuaggelion 'nioudas,* "The Gospel of Judas"—but not "The Gospel According to (*kata* or *pkata*) Judas," as we might expect on the basis of titles of other early Christian gospels. This is not a gospel written by Judas—Judas is not designated, pseudonymously, as the author of the gospel. Rather, this is a gospel about Judas or even for Judas, and his relationship to Jesus and his role in the story of the last days of Jesus are focal points of the gospel.

The *Gospel of Judas* begins with an incipit, or opening, that identifies the text as a "secret revelatory discourse" (33) that Jesus shares with Judas Iscariot shortly before the time of his crucifixion. Following the summary of the career of Jesus, a scene is presented in which Jesus comes upon his disciples as they are celebrating a holy meal together, and he laughs, but he maintains that he is only laughing because of their overly scrupulous desire to do the will of their God. When the disciples profess that Jesus is in fact the son of their God (34), Jesus himself begs to differ: their God, it seems, is the demiurge, the creator of this world, and not the transcendent deity who is exalted over all. The disciples are not pleased by this, but they cannot accept Jesus's invitation to stand before him—with the exception of Judas, who stands in front of Jesus and utters the correct confession of who Jesus is. He says to Jesus, "You have come from the immortal realm (or aeon) of Barbelo, and I am not worthy to pronounce the name of the one who has sent you" (35). In what survives of the *Gospel of Judas,* Barbelo is mentioned only here, but the name Barbelo is well known from other Gnostic sources. In these sources Barbelo functions as the divine Mother or the manifestation of the divine power of the highest God, and thus the confession by Judas may be taken to affirm that Jesus is the son or offspring of the transcendent deity.

In the scenes that follow in the *Gospel of Judas,* Jesus appears several times to speak with the disciples and at times privately with Judas. Much of the conversation between Jesus and his disciples addresses, in one way or another, the various groups of human beings and religious folks that may be distinguished, and Jesus stresses that a particular group of people is especially blessed. This group is said to derive from the realms above and is described in the *Gospel of Judas* as the generation of Seth—or, more concisely, as "that generation," linked to Seth. Here and in other Gnostic texts, the figure of Seth builds upon the tradition of Seth son of Adam and Eve, whose birth, according to *Genesis,* provided a new beginning for humankind following the murder of Abel and the banishment of Cain. In certain Gnostic texts, such as the *Gospel of Judas,* the roles of Adam (or Adamas) and Seth are accentuated; in good Platonic fashion they are depicted not only as earthly characters but also as heavenly figures, and the people of gnosis, the Gnostics, are considered to be the offspring of Seth. Such Gnostic texts are commonly described as Sethian texts by scholars, and the Gnostics who composed and read these texts are frequently referred to as Sethians, on account of the emphasis placed upon Seth and the generation of Seth within the texts. The *Gospel of Judas* is such a text with Sethian influence, and it may be judged, I suggest, to represent an early example of Sethian gnosis.

A key part of the discussion between Jesus and Judas in the *Gospel of Judas* involves Jesus revealing to Judas, at length, the nature of the divine and the way in which the divine extends itself through emanations and manifestations down to our world below (47). The divine light from above shines down into this world, and the transcendent deity—the great invisible Spirit, a phrase used extensively among Sethians to depict the highest deity—comes to expression through the Self-Generated (Autogenes) and a host of heavenly figures, including Adamas and, perhaps, Seth. According to the revelation given to Judas, the heavenly hosts that come to expression number in the myriads, and an assemblage of the entities is termed the cosmos or universe. The cosmos is called "corruption" (50), and demiurgic powers named Nebro, Yaldabaoth, and Sakla (or Saklas), familiar from other Sethian texts, set up a bureaucratic structure and create this world below and human beings in this world (50–53).

Much of this cosmological material in the *Gospel of Judas* recalls accounts, especially Sethian accounts, of the evolution, or devolution, of the divine. Close parallels may be noted between the *Gospel of Judas* and the *Secret Book of John* and the *Holy Book of the Great Invisible Spirit* as well as *Eugnostos the Blessed* and the *Wisdom of Jesus Christ*—all texts from the Nag Hammadi library and the Berlin Gnostic Codex. Sophia, personified Wisdom, who is a primary actress in many accounts of the cosmological drama, is not presented in this revelation of Jesus in the *Gospel of Judas*, although she may be referred to once, earlier in the text, as "corruptible Wisdom" (44). It is possible that Wisdom, or Sophia, may be lurking in a lacuna, but it may be difficult to find much room for her in the available gaps within the text.

Furthermore, except for a single mention of Christ in the cosmological revelation (52), the entire passage (though placed on the lips of Jesus) is reflective of Hellenistic Jewish thought, and it may come from a Sethian Jewish account of the transcendent nature of the divine and the origin of the universe. I submit that a Jewish mystical or Gnostic source may lie behind this section of the *Gospel of Judas*, and Jewish speculation may have been taken over and lightly Christianized as the teaching of Jesus in the *Gospel of Judas*. A similar process seems to have taken place in the composition of the *Secret Book of John*, another Sethian text, and in the development from the Jewish text *Eugnostos the Blessed* to the Christian text entitled the *Wisdom of Jesus Christ*. In the case of the *Gospel of Judas*, the Jewish basis for much of the text may help to account for the similarities, noted in the general introduction, between this section of the *Gospel of Judas* and Jewish mystical traditions, including later Kabbalah. Whether ultimately Jesus himself may be understood as a Jewish mystic and thus may be proposed as the source of some of the mystical material in the *Gospel of Judas* is a question that may merit further exploration.

Finally, Jesus says to Judas, "You will exceed all of them. For you will sacrifice the man who bears me" (56). The practice of sacrifice in general is strongly criticized in the *Gospel of Judas*, and advocates of a sacrificial interpretation of the death of Jesus and the eucharist, such as the leaders of the emerging orthodox church, seem to be accused of sacrificing their own children, apparently a reference to Christian believers in the church. The *Gospel of Judas* thus seems to reject in a vigorous way the belief that Jesus died as a sacrifice for sins and that the salvific death of Jesus should be celebrated in the eucharist—and, as Elaine Pagels and Karen King point out in their book *Reading Judas*, the gospel may likewise deny that Christian believers ought to emulate Jesus by going to their own deaths as martyrs and sacrificing themselves to the authorities. In the present passage of the *Gospel of Judas*, however, a rather different meaning of sacrifice may be introduced: Jesus states that Judas will sacrifice the man—the physical man with the fleshly body—who is the biological basis for the real person of Jesus. In other words, here Jesus appears to indicate that Judas will help the inner person of Jesus—the spiritual person, the true person—become liberated and will turn the man in to the authorities to be executed. Judas Iscariot, often vilified and marginalized in Christian tradition, is restored as an insightful disciple in the *Gospel of Judas*, and here Judas is completely devoted to Jesus. Jesus goes on to remind Judas that he has now been fully informed about spiritual things, and he encourages Judas to look up to the heavenly cloud, the divine light, and the stars and be enlightened.

In presentations at conferences in Paris and Washington, D.C., a few colleagues and friends—April DeConick, Louis Painchaud, and John Turner—have proposed a revisionist understanding of the *Gospel of Judas* based in part on a totally different understanding of this passage from page 56 of the text ("You will exceed all of them. For you will sacrifice the man who bears me"). Rather than presenting a positive image of Judas, they have posited, the *Gospel of Judas* means to portray Judas in a negative light as an evil figure who does an evil deed in betraying Jesus. Admittedly the passage cited from page 56 is in a sentence of the text with lacunae around it, and the context of the quotation is not easy to determine. The alternative interpretation of this passage suggests that Jesus tells Judas he will exceed all the rest, but in evil. Further, it is suggested that if Judas enters a cloud of light, it may be the cloud of the demiurge. Thus, in such an understanding of Judas and the *Gospel of Judas*, poor Judas turns out to be a tragic figure, perhaps even a demon (44), and the message of the *Gospel of Judas* is not really *evangelium*, "good news," but *dysangelium*, "bad news."

Such a tragic rereading of the *Gospel of Judas* is worthy of consideration as an alternative understanding of the text, but it may be difficult to sustain without considerable qualification. Time, and scholarly discussion, will tell. In order to buy into this reinterpretation of the figure of Judas in the *Gospel of Judas*, one may need to (1) skip over the incipit, or opening of the text, with its announcement of the nature of the text and the relationship between Jesus and Judas in it, as well as the title, with its indication that the text announces good news; (2) ignore all the instances in which Judas professes Jesus correctly, is taught the mysteries of the kingdom by Jesus, and is commended by Jesus; (3) impose passages from later Sethian texts (regarding, for instance, the thirteenth aeon and its connection with the demiurge) upon what is most likely an early example of Sethian Gnostic thought; and (4) employ fairly tendentious interpretations of passages in the gospel in order to argue against what seems to be the plain sense of the preserved text.

In November 2006, at the same Washington conference, another colleague, Ismo Dunderberg, offered a more nuanced interpretation of the concluding portion of the *Gospel of Judas*. In the gospel, after Jesus says to Judas, "You will sacrifice the man who bears me," there are four lines that recall statements from the *Psalms* in the Jewish Scriptures, and these lines seem to indicate the strength of spirit that is necessary if Judas is going to be able to hand

Jesus over to the authorities. Dunderberg observed that the lines could be taken in a negative sense, to be sure, but that in actuality the text may be admitting that Judas must have emotional strength and boldness if he is to accomplish what Jesus declares he will do.

To be sure, the final fate of Judas according to the *Gospel of Judas* remains somewhat uncertain, largely on account of missing text at the conclusion of the narrative. It seems most likely that Judas is enlightened and exalted, and that he becomes, for readers of the gospel, a Gnostic paradigm of discipleship and faithfulness to Jesus. It is possible, I would grant, that Judas may not attain ultimate bliss in the *Gospel of Judas.* Or he may be on his way to the thirteenth eternal realm, to dominate the powers of the world from there, as Gregor Wurst has guessed. Yet what is clear from the text is the positive role of the disciple Judas, who, though opposed by the other disciples, understands who Jesus is, learns the mysteries of the kingdom from Jesus, and does what Jesus says he will do.

Thus, the *Gospel of Judas* comes to a close with the act of Judas handing Jesus over to the high priests and scholars. The text does not include a passion narrative or any account of the crucifixion of Jesus. The last words of the gospel read, "And Judas received some money and handed him over to them" (58). That, as I read it, is a main point of the gospel. Judas, the disciple closest to Jesus, remains loyal to Jesus to the end.

The English translation of the *Gospel of Judas* presented here must remain somewhat provisional (see the notes for additional readings), and we would anticipate that further restorations, reconstructions, and interpretations of this challenging text will be offered by colleagues during the coming years.

THE GOSPEL OF JUDAS[1]

Opening

The secret revelatory discourse that Jesus spoke with Judas Iscariot in the course of a week,[2] three days before his passion.[3]

The Life of Jesus

When he appeared on the earth, he performed signs and great wonders for the salvation of humankind. Some [walked] on the path of justice, but others stumbled in their mistakes, and so the twelve disciples were called.[4]

He began to discuss with them the mysteries that transcend the world and what will happen at the end. Many a time he does not appear as himself to his disciples, but you find him as a child among them.[5]

Jesus Discusses the Prayer of Thanksgiving

Now, one day he was with his disciples in Judea, and he happened upon them as they were assembled together, seated and practicing their piety. When he [drew] near to his disciples [34] as they were assembled together, seated and giving thanks[6] over the bread, [he] laughed.[7]

The disciples said to [him], "Master, why are you laughing at [our] prayer of thanksgiving?[8] What is it we have done? This is what is proper."

He answered and said to them, "I'm not laughing at you. You aren't doing this out of your own will, but because in this way your God [will be] praised."

They said, "Master, you are . . . the son of our God."[9]

Jesus said to them, "How is it that you know me? [I] tell you the truth,[10] no generation will know me among the people who are with you."

The Disciples Are Angry

When his disciples heard this, [they] began getting angry and hostile and blaspheming against him in their minds.

Jesus recognized that they did not [understand, and he said] to them, "Why has your concern produced this hostility? Your god who is within you and [his powers][11] [35] have become angry within your souls.[12] [Let] any of you who is a [strong enough] person bring forward the perfect human being and stand before my face."

They all said, "We are strong."

But none of their spirits dared to stand before [him], except Judas Iscariot. He was able to stand before him, yet he could not look him in the eye, but he turned his face away.[13]

Judas [said] to him, "I know who you are and from what place you have come. You have come from the immortal realm[14] of Barbelo,[15] and I am not worthy to pronounce the name of the one who has sent you."[16]

Jesus Speaks Privately with Judas

Jesus understood that Judas[17] was contemplating things that are lofty, and he said to him, "Move away from the others, and I shall explain to you the mysteries of the kingdom, not so that you will attain it, but you will go[18] through a great deal of grief.[19] [36] For somebody else will take your place, so that the twelve [disciples] may be complete once again with their God."[20]

Judas said to him, "When will you explain these things to me? And [how][21] will the great day of light dawn for the ... generation?"

But when he said these things, Jesus departed from him.

Jesus Appears to the Disciples Again

The next day, in the morning, he [appeared] to his disciples.

They said to him, "Master, where did [you] go and what did you do when you departed from us?"

Jesus said to them, "I went to a different generation, one that is great and holy."

His disciples said to him, "Lord,[22] what is the great generation that is exalted over us and is holy, but is not present in these realms?"[23]

When Jesus heard these things, he laughed and said to them, "Why are you reflecting in your minds about the generation that is powerful and holy? [37]

[I] tell you the truth,[24]
no one born [of] this realm[25] *will behold that [generation],*
no angelic host of the stars[26] *will rule over that generation,*
no human of mortal birth will be able to accompany it,
because that generation is not from . . .
that has come to be . . . .
The generation of people among [you]
is from the generation of humanity . . .
power, which . . .
powers . . .
[through] which you rule."

When [his] disciples heard these things, each one was troubled in spirit. They were speechless.

Jesus Appears Again

On another day Jesus approached [them]. They said to [him], "Master, we have had a [vision] of you, for we saw [dreams] of great power[27] last night."

[He said], "Why have [you] . . . and hidden yourselves away?"[28] [38]

The Disciples Behold the Temple

They [said, "We have] seen a huge [house[29] in which there was a] great altar, and twelve men—they were priests, we would say— and a name.[30] A crowd was in attendance at that altar,[31] [until] the priests [were done presenting] the offerings. We [also] were in attendance."

[Jesus said], "What kind of people are [the priests]?"

They [said, "Some abstain³² for] two weeks. [Some] sacrifice their own children, others their wives, while praising and acting humbly with each other. Some have sex with men. Some perform acts of [murder]. Some commit all sorts of sins and lawless deeds. And the men who stand [before] the altar call upon your [name], [39] and through all the actions of their deficiency,³³ that [altar] becomes full."³⁴

After they said these things, they became silent, since they were upset.

Jesus's Allegorical Interpretation of the Temple

Jesus said to them, "Why are you upset? I tell you the truth,³⁵ all the priests who stand at that altar call upon my name. I tell you again, my name has been written on the . . . of the generations of the stars through the generations of people. They have planted trees in my name, without fruit, in a shameful way."³⁶

Jesus said to them, "You are the ones presenting the offerings at the altar you have seen. That is the God you serve, and you are the twelve men you have seen. And the cattle brought in are the offerings you have seen—they are the multitude you lead astray [40] before that altar. [The ruler of this world]³⁷ will stand and use my name in this manner, and generations of pious people will cling to him. After him another man will come forward from [those who are immoral],³⁸ and another [will] come from the child-killers, and another from those who have sex with men, and those who abstain,[39] and the rest of those who are impure and lawless and prone to error, as well as those who say, 'We are like angels'; they are the stars that bring everything to its end. For to the generations of people it has been said, 'Look, God has received your offering from the hands of the priests,'[40] that is, a minister of error. But it is the Lord who commands who is the Lord of all.[41] On the last day they will be put to shame." [41]

Jesus said [to them], "Stop [sacrificing] . . . that you have . . . on the altar, since they are over your stars and your angels and they have already come to their end there. So let them be . . .[42] before you, and let them go . . . . . .[43] generations . . . . A baker cannot feed all of creation [42] that is under [heaven]."

And [when the disciples heard these things], they said to [him], ". . . us and . . . ."

Jesus said to them, "Stop disputing with me. Each of you has your own star,[44] and everyone . . . . . .[45] [43] in . . . that has not come . . . [spring of water] for the tree . . . of this realm[46] . . . after a while . . . but that one[47] has come to provide water for[48] the paradise of God, and the [race][49] that will endure, because [that one] will not defile the [way of life of] that generation, but . . . from eternity to eternity."

Jesus and Judas Discuss the Generations of People

Judas said to [him, "Rabbi],[50] what fruit is it that this generation produces?"

Jesus said, "The souls of all generations of people will die. When these people, however, bring the time of the kingdom to completion and the spirit parts from them, their bodies will die, but their souls will be alive and will be taken up."

Judas said, "And what will the rest of the generations of people do?"

Jesus said, "Nobody can [44] sow seed[51] on [rock] and harvest its produce.[52] This is also how . . . the [defiled] race[53] and corruptible Wisdom[54] . . . the hand that created mortal people, and their souls ascend to the eternal realms[55] on high. I tell you the [truth,[56] there is no authority] or angel [or] power that will be able to behold those [realms] that [this great], holy generation [will behold]."

After Jesus said these things, he went off.

Jesus and Judas Discuss a Vision

Judas said, "Master, just as you have listened to all of them, now also listen to me. For I have seen a powerful vision."

Jesus heard this and laughed, and he said to him, "O thirteenth spirit,[57] why are you so excited? Speak your mind, then, and I'll hear you out."

Judas said to him, "I have seen myself in the vision as the twelve disciples were stoning me and [45] treating [me harshly]. And I also came to the place that . . . after you. I saw [a house] . . . , and my eyes could not [grasp] its dimensions. Important people moved around it. That house <had> a thatched roof,[58] and within the house there was [a crowd] . . . . . . ,[59] 'Master, let me also come in with these people.'"

[Jesus] answered and said, "Your star has deceived you, Judas. Further,

No person of mortal birth is worthy
to go into the house you have seen:
that place is kept for the saints,[60]
where sun and moon will not rule,
nor the day,
but they will stand there always
in the eternal realm[61] with the holy angels.

"Look, I have told you the mysteries of the kingdom [46] and I have taught you the error of the stars, and . . . send . . . on the twelve realms."[62]

Judas Asks About His Own Fate

Judas said, "Master, is it possible that my seed is subject to the rulers?"[63]

Jesus answered and said to him, "Come, that I may . . . [you, that] . . . . . . ,[64] but you will go[65] through a great deal of grief when you see the kingdom and its entire generation."

When Judas heard these things, he said to him, "What advantage is there for me,[66] since you have set me apart for[67] that generation?"

Jesus answered and said, "You will be the thirteenth, and you will be cursed by the other generations, but eventually you will rule[68] over them. In the last days they will . . . to you, that you may not ascend[69] up [47] to the holy [generation]."

Jesus Teaches Judas About the Divine and the Universe

Jesus said, "[Come], that I may teach you about the things . . . [that] no person will see.[70] For there is a great and infinite realm,[71] whose dimensions no angelic generation could see, [in] which is the[72] great invisible [Spirit],[73]

> which no eye of angel has seen,
> no thought of the mind has grasped,
> nor was it called by a name.[74]

"And a cloud of light appeared in that place. And he[75] said, 'Let an angel come into existence as my attendant.'[76]

"And a great angel, the Self-Generated, God of light, came from the cloud. Four more angels came into existence because of him, from another cloud, and they served as attendants for the angelic Self-Generated.[77] And the Self-Generated said, [48] 'Let [Adamas] come into existence,' and [the emanation] came to be. And he [created] the first luminary to rule over him. And he said, 'Let angels come into existence, for adoration [of him],' and ten thousands without number came to be. And he said, '[Let] an eternal being[78] of light come into existence,' and he came to be. He established the second luminary [to] rule over him, with ten thousands of angels without number, for adoration. This is how he created the rest of the eternal beings[79] of light, and he made them rule over them. And he created for them ten thousands of angels without number, for assistance.

Adamas, Luminaries, Heavens, Firmaments

"Adamas was in the first cloud of light, which no angel could see among all those who are called 'God.' And he [49] . . . that . . . [after] the image . . . and after the likeness of [this] angel, he revealed the incorruptible [generation] of Seth . . . the twelve . . . twenty-four . . . . He revealed seventy-two luminaries in the incorruptible generation, by the will of the Spirit. The seventy-two luminaries in turn revealed three hundred sixty luminaries in the incorruptible generation, by the will of the Spirit, so that their number would be five for each.

"Their father consists of the twelve eternal beings[80] of the twelve luminaries, and for each eternal being there are six heavens, so that there are seventy-two heavens for the seventy-two luminaries, and for each [50] [of them five] firmaments, [in order that there might be] three hundred sixty [firmaments]. They were given authority and a [great] angelic host [without number], for honor and adoration, [and in addition] virgin spirits [as well],[81] for honor and [adoration] of all the eternal beings[82] and the heavens and their firmaments.[83]

Cosmos, Chaos, Underworld

"Now, the multitude of those immortal beings is called 'cosmos,' that is, corruption, through the Father and the seventy-two luminaries with the Self-Generated and his seventy-two eternal beings.[84] There[85] the first human appeared, with his incorruptible powers. The eternal being[86] that appeared with his generation, the one in whom are the cloud of knowledge[87] and the angel, is called [51] El.[88] . . . realm . . .

"After these things . . . said, 'Let twelve angels come into existence [to] rule over chaos and the [underworld].' And look, from the cloud an [angel] appeared, whose face blazed with fire[89] and whose countenance was fouled with blood.[90] His name was Nebro,[91] which is interpreted as 'rebel,' but others name him Yaldabaoth. And another angel, Sakla,[92] also came from the cloud. So Nebro created six angels, with Sakla, to be attendants, and these produced twelve angels in the heavens, and each one received a share in the heavens.[93]

Rulers and Angels

"And the twelve rulers[94] talked to the twelve angels: 'Let each of you [52] . . . and let them . . . generation . . . . . .[95] [five] angels.'

> The first is [Se]th, who is called Christ.
> The [second] is Harmathoth, who is . . . .
> The [third] is Galila.
> The fourth is Yobel.
> The fifth is Adonaios.

These are the five who ruled over the underworld, and are first over chaos.[96]

The Creation of Humanity

"Then Sakla said to his angels, 'Let's create a human being after the likeness and after the image.'[97] They formed Adam and his partner Eve, who in the cloud is called Zoe. For all the generations seek him under this name, but each of them calls her with their own names. Now, Sakla[98] did not [53] [command] . . . except . . . the generations . . . this . . . . And the [ruler][99] said to him, 'Your life is extended for a time, along with your children.'"

Jesus and Judas Discuss the Destiny of Adam and Humanity

Judas said to Jesus, "[What] is the length of time that the human being will live?"

Jesus said, "Why are you concerned about this, that Adam, along with his generation, has received the length of his life with a designated period of time,[100] in the place where he has received his kingdom, with a designated period of time with his ruler?"[101]

Judas said to Jesus, "Does the human spirit die?"

Jesus said, "This is the reason why God commanded Michael to give the spirits of people to them on loan, for adoration, but the Great One commanded Gabriel to give spirits to the great generation without a king[102]—the spirit and the soul. Therefore, the [rest] of the souls [54] . . . .[103]

Jesus Discusses the Destruction of the Wicked with Judas and Others

". . . light . . . . . .[104] around . . . spirit within you,[105] [which] you have made to dwell in this [flesh] among the generations of angels. But God caused knowledge[106] to be [granted] to Adam and those who are with him, so that the kings of chaos and the underworld might not dominate them."

Judas said to Jesus, "Then what will those generations do?"

Jesus said, "I tell you[107] the truth,[108] the stars above all bring matters to their end. When Sakla completes his time designated for him, their first star will shine with the generations, and they will bring to completion what has been mentioned. Then they will do immoral things[109] in my name and slay their children, [55] and they will . . . and . . . . . .[110] [in] my name, and[111] your star will rule over the [thir]teenth eternal realm."[112]

And afterward Jesus [laughed].

[Judas said], "Master, [why are you laughing at us]?"

[Jesus] answered [and said], "I'm not laughing [at you] but rather at the error of the stars, because these six stars wander around with these five warriors, and all of them will be destroyed, with their creatures."[113]

Jesus Speaks of the Baptized, and of Judas's Act of Handing Him Over

Judas said to Jesus, "Those who have been baptized in your name, then, what will they do?"

Jesus said, "I tell [you] the truth,[114] this baptism [56] . . . [in] my name . . . . . .[115] to me. [I] tell you the truth,[116] Judas, those [who] bring sacrifices to Sakla . . . God . . . . . .[117] everything evil.

"But you will exceed all of them.[118] For you will sacrifice the man who bears me.[119]

> Already your horn has been lifted up,
> and your anger has flared up,
> and your star has burned brightly,[120]
> and your heart[121] has [grown strong].[122] [57]

"[I tell you] the truth,[123] your last [days] . . . become . . . . . .[124] grieve . . . . . .[125] the ruler,[126] since he will be overthrown. And then the image of the great generation of Adam will be magnified, for before heaven, earth, and the angels, that generation from the eternal realms[127] exists.

"Look, you have been informed of everything. Lift up your eyes and behold the cloud and the light that is within it and the stars that are circling it. And the star that leads the way is your star."

Transfiguration

Judas lifted up his eyes and beheld the cloud of light, and he[128] entered it. Those who were standing on the ground heard a voice coming from the cloud and saying, [58] . . . great generation . . . image . . . and . . . .[129]

Conclusion: Judas Hands Jesus Over

. . . [Now], their high priests murmured because [he][130] had stepped into the guest room[131] for his prayer. But some scholars were there watching closely in order to lay hold of him during the prayer, for they were afraid of the people, since he was regarded by them all as a prophet.

And they came over to Judas and said to him, "What are you doing in this place? You are Jesus's disciple."

He answered them in accordance with their wish.

And Judas received some money and handed him over[132] to them.

The Gospel of Judas[133]

CHAPTER THREE

Judas in the
Dialogue of the Savior

THE *DIALOGUE OF THE SAVIOR* IS, AS THE TITLE OF THE TEXT suggests, a dialogue in which Jesus and his disciples converse together. The discussion in the *Dialogue of the Savior* focuses upon a variety of different themes, many of them having to do with the life of gnosis. This text is preserved as the fifth tractate in Nag Hammadi Codex III, and although the state of the preservation of the papyrus document is not good, much of it can be restored with a reasonable degree of confidence. Like the *Gospel of Judas*, the *Dialogue of the Savior* was probably composed in the second century CE. Also like the *Gospel of Judas*, the *Dialogue of the Savior* is centrally concerned about things Gnostic, and the text encourages readers to seek after knowledge. As the Master Jesus says in *Dialogue of the Savior* 129, "Let one who [knows] seek and find and rejoice."

The *Dialogue of the Savior* was most likely written on the basis of several earlier sources, and Helmut Koester and Elaine Pagels identify five such sources that they believe have shaped the character of the text: (1) a dialogue between the Master Jesus and his disciples, with sayings of Jesus that recall portions of the *Gospel of Thomas* (124ff.); (2) part of a creation story (127–31); (3) a list of wisdom observations with cosmological features (133–34); (4) part of an apocalyptic vision (134–37); and (5) an introduction about Jesus, called the Savior, that is added at the opening of the text (120–24).

The *Dialogue of the Savior* begins with the Savior Jesus addressing the disciples. He says, "Now the time has come, brothers and sisters, for us to leave our labor behind and stand at rest, for whoever stands at rest will rest forever" (120). Jesus offers a prayer of praise, and then he proceeds to teach the disciples about the end of all things in a section of the text that has, unfortunately, numerous lacunae. The dialogue that ensues allows Jesus and his disciples to explore a number of topics, including the inner life, spirit and body, light and darkness, creation and the word, fire and water, the world and the rulers of the world, fullness and deficiency—all matters of life and death well known from Gnostic texts.

Within the dialogue the disciple Mary—usually thought to be identified with Mary Magdalene, a close disciple of Jesus in many Gnostic texts—is singled out for particular praise. When she pronounces three wisdom sayings, she is acknowledged for her understanding, and the text declares, "She spoke this utterance as a woman who understood everything" (139). The point of the inquiry into knowledge in the *Dialogue of the Savior* is salvation, and, Jesus explains, those who seek and find discover that the spiritual reality bringing ultimate joy is within. Jesus says, "I tell you [the truth], look, what you seek and inquire about [is] within you, and it [has] the power and mystery [of the] spirit, for [it is] from [the spirit]" (128).

Three disciples are mentioned by name in the *Dialogue of the Savior* and given special attention as partners in discussion with Jesus. One, Mary, is probably to be identified, as already noted, with Mary Magdalene, whose prominent role in the *Gospel of Mary,* the *Gospel of Thomas,* the *Gospel of Philip, Pistis Sophia,* and the *Manichaean Psalm Book* (to say nothing of the New Testament gospels) is well known. A second disciple is named Matthew (*Maththaios*), and he may be understood to be the disciple (*Matthaios* or *Maththaios*) in the circle of the Twelve, the replacement disciple (*Matthias* or *Maththias*) who assumed the position after the departure of Judas Iscariot according to *Acts* 1, or the scribe (*Mathaias*) mentioned at the opening of the *Book of Thomas* as the recorder of the hidden sayings the Savior spoke to Judas Thomas—or he may simply be a composite of characters named Matthew.

The third disciple in the *Dialogue of the Savior* is Judas. Judas is mentioned no fewer than twenty times in the extant pages of the *Dialogue of the Savior* (125; 127; 129; 131; 132; 134; 135 [twice]; 138 [four times]; 140; 142; 143; 144; 145; 146 [three times]; cf. also the possible restoration of his name on page 128). Judas in the *Dialogue of the Savior* has usually been identified with Judas Thomas, the twin brother of Jesus, since Judas Thomas is also deeply involved with sayings of Jesus in such texts as the *Gospel of Thomas* and the *Book of Thomas.* Further, the parallels between sayings of Jesus in the *Dialogue of the Savior* and his sayings in the *Gospel of Thomas* may also lead us to suppose that in the present text Judas is assumed to be Judas

Thomas. Yet the publication of the *Gospel of Judas* now leaves open the possibility that the Judas who figures as a leading disciple in the *Dialogue of the Savior* could be Judas Iscariot.

In the *Dialogue of the Savior,* Judas functions as an inquirer into profound issues and a visionary who is led by Jesus to a comprehension of the universe. Although we cannot be sure of the identity of Judas in the *Dialogue of the Savior,* much of this presentation of Judas coheres, in general, with the depiction of Judas Iscariot in the *Gospel of Judas.* Thus, in the *Dialogue of the Savior,* Judas asks the Master Jesus about soul and spirit and what existed at the beginning, and he comments on how "all things are [just] like signs over [the earth]" (129). He also bows down and praises Jesus. He inquires about earthquakes, rulers, and bodily garments, and he wonders about living and dying, the beginning of the way, and how to pray. In the discussion he observes, concerning the world of birth and mortality, "The works of the [female] will perish. [Then] the rulers will [call upon their realms], and we shall be ready for them" (145). Along with Mary and Matthew, Judas is granted a vision of heaven and earth, and he beholds what is above and what is below. Near the end of the text Judas engages in a quick set of exchanges with Jesus about how the spirit is disclosed, how the light is disclosed, and what forgiveness means for the world and the works of people—to which Jesus responds, "Who [knows]? For it is the responsibility of whoever has come to know the works to do the [will] of the Father" (146). In all these instances Judas—whether Judas Thomas or Judas Iscariot—proves to be a worthy disciple and a good friend of his Master, Jesus.

THE DIALOGUE OF THE SAVIOR[1]

The Savior Teaches About Rest

The Savior said to his disciples, "Now the time has come, brothers and sisters,[2] for us to leave our labor[3] behind and stand at rest,[4] for whoever stands at rest will rest forever. I say to you, always rise above . . . time . . . . [I say] to you, . . . [do not] be afraid of [those] . . . you. I [say to you], anger is frightening, [and whoever] stirs up anger is a [frightening person]. But since you have [been able to endure], it may come from [you] . . . .

"People received these words about anger[5] with fear and trembling. Anger established rulers over them, for no one escapes anger. But when I came, I opened a path and taught people about the way of passage for those who are chosen and alone,[6] [121] who have known the Father and have believed the truth. And you offered praise.

Giving Praise to the Father

"Now, when you offer praise, do so in this way:

Hear us, Father,
as you have heard your only Son
and have received him to yourself.[7]
[You have] given him rest from many [labors].
Your power is [invincible],
[because] your armaments are [invincible],

. . . light . . . alive . . . inaccessible . . . [alive].
The [true] word [8] *[has brought] repentance for life,*
[and this has come] from you.
You are the thought and supreme serenity
of those who are alone. [9]
Again, hear us
as you have heard your chosen.
Through your sacrifice the chosen will enter.
Through their good works they have freed their souls
from blind bodily limbs,
so that they may come to be [122] forever.
Amen.

Overcoming the Power of Darkness

"I shall teach you. At the time of destruction the first power of darkness will come upon you. Do not be afraid and say, 'Look, the time has come.' But when you see a single staff . . . understand that . . . from some such thing . . . and the rulers . . . come upon you . . . . In truth, fear is the power [of darkness]. So if you are afraid of what is about to come upon you, it will overwhelm you, and not one among them will spare you or show you mercy. Rather, look at [what is] within, since you have mastered every word on earth. This [123] [will] take you up to a [place] where there is no dominion [and no] tyrant. When you . . . you will see those . . . and you will also [hear them. I] tell you, reflection . . . . Reflection is . . . [where] truth [is] . . . but they . . . and you . . . truth. This [is . . . in] living [mind]. Therefore . . . and your joy . . . in order that . . . your souls . . . lest the word . . . which they raised . . . and they could not [understand] it . . . . Make what is [inside] you and what is [outside you a single one].[10] To be sure, the place [124] of crossing is frightening in [your] sight, but without hesitation pass by.[11] Its depth is great, [its] height [is] staggering. [Be of a single mind] . . . and the fire . . . dew drops . . . all powers . . . you. They will . . . and [all] powers . . . they . . . in front. I tell [you], . . . the soul . . . becomes . . . in each one . . . you are . . . and that . . . sleep not . . . the children . . . and you . . . you . . . ."

The Savior and His Disciples Discuss the Inner Life

Matthew[12] said, "How . . . ?" [125]

The Savior said, "[If you do not keep] what is within you [in order, your work] will remain, but you [will not]."

Judas[13] [said], "Master,[14] [I want to understand all] the works of the souls [that are in] these little ones. When . . . , where will they be? . . . the spirit . . . ?"

The Master [said, ". . . receive] them. They do not die and are not destroyed, because they have known [their] companions and the one who will receive them. For truth seeks the wise and the righteous."

The Savior [said], "The lamp [of the] body is the mind. As long as [what is within] you is kept in order—that is, [the soul][15]—your bodies are [enlightened]. As long as your hearts are dark, your light, which you [126] expect, [is far from you].[16] I have called [you to myself], since I am about to depart, so that [you may receive] my word among [yourselves. Look], I am sending it to [you]."[17]

Who Seeks, Who Reveals?

His disciples [said, "Master], who seeks and [who] reveals?"

[The Master] said [to them], "One who seeks [also] reveals."

Matthew [said to him again, "Master], when I [listen to you] and I speak, who is it who [speaks and] who listens?"

The [Master] said, "One who speaks also [listens], and one who can see also reveals."

Mary[18] said, "Master, look, [while I] wear a body, where do my tears come from, where does my laughter come from?"

The Master said, "[The body] weeps because of its works [and what] remains to be done. The mind laughs [because of [127] the fruits[19] of] the spirit. Whoever does not [stand] in darkness will [not] be able to see [the light].[20] I tell you, [what has no] light is darkness, [and whoever does not] stand in [darkness will] not [be able] to see the light. [The children of] falsehood, however, were taken out . . . . You will put on light, and [so you will live] forever . . . . [If] . . . ,[21] then [all] the powers above and below will treat you harshly. In that place [there will] be weeping and [gnashing] of teeth over the end of all."

The Creation of the World

Judas said, "Tell [us], Master, what [existed] before [heaven and] earth came into being?"[22]

The Master said, "There was darkness and water, and [128] spirit upon [water].[23] And I tell you [the truth], look, what you seek and inquire about [is] within you, and it [has] the power and mystery [of the] spirit, for [it is] from [the spirit].[24] Wickedness entered [in order to destroy] the mind, [forever]. Look . . . ."[25]

[Matthew] said,[26] "Master, tell us, where is [the soul] established and where does the true [mind] dwell?"

The Master [said], "The fire of the spirit came into existence
[between] the two, and so there came to be [spirit][27] and the true
mind within them. [If] someone establishes the soul on high,
then [the person will] be exalted."

Seek, Find, Rejoice

Matthew asked him [129], "[Isn't . . .[28] necessary], when it is understood [in the true sense]?"[29]

The Master [said, ". . . is] more useful than your [work. Re-
move] from yourselves [what can] pursue you and everything [in]
your hearts. For as your hearts . . . ,[30] so [will you find] a way
to overcome the powers above and below. And I say to you, let
one [who has] power renounce [it and] repent,[31] and let one who
[knows] seek and find and rejoice."[32]

Judas said, "Look, [I] see that all things are [just] like signs
over [the earth], and that is why they have come to be in this way."

The Emergence of the Word

The Master [said], "When the Father established the world, he
[collected] some of its water, and the word[33] came from it. [130]
It[34] experienced many [troubles, but] it was more exalted than the
path [of the stars] around the entire earth."[35]

[He continued],[36] "The water collected [above] is beyond the
stars, and [beyond] the water <is> a great fire encircling them like
a wall. Periods of time [began to be measured] once many of the
beings [that] were within had separated from the rest.

"When the [word] was established, he looked [down]. The Father said to him, 'Go, [send[37] something] from yourself, so that [the earth] may not be in want from generation to [generation and] from age to age.'

"So [he] sent[38] from himself fountains of milk, fountains of honey, oil, wine, and fine fruit and delicious flavors and sound roots, [so that] the earth might not be deficient from generation [to] generation and from age to age.

"The word is above . . . [131] stood [and showed] his beauty . . . . And outside [was a great light], brighter [than] the one like it,[39] for that one rules over [all] the realms above and below. [Light was] taken from the fire and dispersed in the [firmament][40] above and below. Those over the heaven above and the earth below depend upon them. Everything is dependent upon them."

When Judas heard this, he bowed down, fell on his knees,[41] and praised the Master.

The Savior and His Disciples Discuss the Place of Life

Mary asked her brothers, "Where are you going to store [these] questions you ask of the Son of [Humanity]?"[42]

The Master [said] to her, "Sister, [no one] can ask about these things [except] someone who has a place [132] to store them in the heart. And such a person can leave [the world] and enter the place [of life], and will not be held back in this world of poverty."[43]

Matthew said, "Master, I want [to see] that place of life, [where] there is no wickedness but only pure light."

The Master replied, "Brother Matthew, you will not be able to see it as [long as you] wear flesh."

Matthew said, "Master, [if I] cannot see it, at least let me understand it."

The Master said, "Everyone who has known oneself [44] has seen oneself. Everything that person is given to do that person does. So such a person has come to [resemble] that place[45] in goodness."[46]

How Does an Earthquake Shake?

Judas answered and said, "Tell me, Master, how does an [earthquake] shake when it shakes the earth?"

The Master picked up a stone and held it in his hand. [He [133] said to him, "What] am I holding in my hand?"

He answered, "[It is] a stone."

He said to them, "What supports the [earth] is also what supports heaven. When a word comes from the Majesty, it will go to what supports heaven and earth. The earth does not move. If it moved, it would collapse. But it does not, so that the first word might not fail. The word established the world and dwelled in it and smelled the fragrance from it.[47] I make known to you, all you children of humanity, all [the things] that do not move, for you are from that place. You live in the hearts of those who speak out in joy and truth. If the word comes from the Father's body, among people, and they do not receive it, it will return back to its place."

Coming to Understanding

"Whoever does [not] know the work of perfection does not know anything.

"One who does not stand in the darkness cannot see the [134] light.

"One who does not [understand] how fire came to be will burn in it, not knowing its origin.[48]

"One who does not first understand water knows nothing. For what use is there for such a person to be baptized in it?

"One who does not understand how the wind that blows came to be will blow away with it.[49]

"One who does not understand how the body that a person wears came to be will perish with it.

"How will someone who does not know the Son know the [Father]?

"All things are hidden from one who does not know the root of all things.

"Whoever does not know the root of wickedness is no stranger to it.

"Those who do not understand how they came will not understand how they will go, and they are no strangers to this world, which will [exalt itself] and be humbled."

Judas, Matthew, and Mary Have an Apocalyptic Vision

He [took] Judas, Matthew, and Mary [135] [to show them the final] consummation of heaven and earth, and when he placed his [hand] on them, they hoped they might [see] it. Judas gazed up and saw a region of great height, and he saw the region of the abyss below.

Judas said to Matthew, "Brother, who can ascend to such a height or descend to the abyss below? For there is great fire there, and great terror."

At that moment a word[50] issued from the height. As Judas was standing there, he saw how the word came [down].

He asked the word, "Why have you come down?"

The Son of Humanity greeted them and said to them, "A seed from a power was deficient, and it descended to the earth's abyss. The Majesty remembered [it] and sent the [word to] it. The word brought the seed up into [the presence] of the Majesty, so that [136] the first word might not be lost."[51]

[His] disciples marveled at everything he told them, and they accepted all of it in faith. And they understood that it was no longer necessary to keep an eye on evil.

Then he said to his disciples, "Didn't I tell you that, like a visible flash of thunder and lightning, what is good will be taken up to the light?"

All his disciples praised him and said, "Master, before you appeared here, who was there to praise you, for all praises are because of you? Or who was there to bless [you], for all blessing comes from you?"

As they were standing there, he saw two spirits bringing a single soul with them, and there was a great flash of lightning. A word came from the Son of Humanity, saying, "Give them their garments," and the small became like the great. They were [like] those who were received up; [137] [there was no distinction] among them.[52]

The [words] he [spoke convinced the] disciples.

Mary Asks About the Vision

Mary [said to him, "Look, I] see the evil [that affects] people from the start, when they dwell with each other."

The Master said [to her], "When you see them, [you under-stand] a great deal; they will [not stay there]. But when you see the one who exists eternally, that is the great vision."

They all said to him, "Explain it to us."

He said to them, "How do you wish to see it, [in] a passing vision or in an eternal vision?"

He went on to say, "Do your best to save what can come after [me], and seek it and speak through it, so that whatever you seek may be in harmony with you. For I [say] to you, truly the living God [is] in you, [138] [as you also are] in God."[53]

Judas Asks About the Rulers of the World and the Garments

Judas [said], "I really want [to learn everything]."

The [Master] said to him, "The living [God does not] dwell [in this] entire [region] of deficiency."[54]

Judas [asked], "Who [will rule over us]?"

The Master replied, "[Look, here are] all the things that exist [among] what remains. You [rule] over them."

Judas said, "But look, the rulers[55] are over us, so they will rule over us."

The Master answered, "You will rule over them. When you re-move jealousy from yourselves, you will clothe yourselves in light and enter the bridal chamber."[56]

Judas asked, "How will [our] garments be brought to us?"

The Master answered, "There are some who will provide them for you and others who will receive [them], [139] and they [will give] you your garments. For who can reach that place? It is very [frightening]. But the garments of life were given to these people because they know the way they will go.[57] Indeed, it is even difficult for me to reach it."[58]

Mary Utters Words of Wisdom

Mary said, "So,

> *The wickedness of each day <is sufficient>.*[59]
> *Workers deserve their food.*[60]
> *Disciples resemble their teachers."* [61]

She spoke this utterance as a woman who understood everything.[62]

The Disciples Ask About Fullness and Deficiency, Life and Death

The disciples asked him, "What is fullness and what is deficiency?"

He answered them, "You are from fullness, and you are in a place of deficiency. And look, his light has poured down on me."

Matthew asked, "Tell me, Master, how the dead die and how the living live." [140]

The Master said, "[You have] asked me about a [true] saying that eye has not seen, nor have I heard it, except from you.[63] But I say to you, when what moves a person slips away, that person will be called dead, and when what is living leaves what is dead, it will be called alive."

Judas asked, "So why, really, do some <die> and some live?"

The Master said, "Whatever is from truth does not die. Whatever is from woman dies."[64]

Mary asked, "Tell me, Master, why have I come to this place, to gain or to lose?"[65]

The Master replied, "You show the abundance of the one who reveals."

Mary asked him, "Master, then is there a place that is abandoned or without truth?"

The Master said, "The place where I am not."

Mary said, "Master, you are awesome and marvelous, [141] and [like a devouring fire] to those who do not know [you]."

Matthew asked, "Why don't we go to our rest at once?"[66]

The Master said, "When you leave these burdens behind."

Matthew asked, "How does the small unite with the great?"

The Master said, "When you leave behind what cannot accompany you, then you will rest."[67]

Mary, Judas, and the Other Disciples Discuss True Life with the Master

Mary said, "I want to understand all things, [just as] they are."

The Master said, "Whoever seeks life, this is their wealth. For the world's [rest] is false, and its gold and silver are deceptive."[68]

His disciples asked him, "What should we do for our work to be perfect?"

The Master [said] to them, "Be ready, in every circumstance. Blessed are they who have found [142] the [strife and have seen] the struggle with their eyes. They have not killed nor have [they] been killed, but they have emerged victorious."

Judas asked, "Tell me, Master, what is the beginning of the way?"[69]

He said, "Love and goodness. If one of these had existed among the rulers, wickedness would never have come to be."

Matthew said, "Master, you have spoken of the end of the universe with no difficulty."

The Master said, "You have understood all the things I said to you, and you have accepted them in faith. If you know them, they are yours. If not, they are not yours."

They asked him, "To what place are we going?"

The Master said, "Stand in the place you can reach."

Mary asked, "Is everything established in this way visible?"

The Master said, "I have told you, the one who can see reveals."

His twelve disciples asked him, "Teacher, [with] [143] serenity . . . teach us . . . ."

The Master said, "[If you have understood] everything I have [told you], you will [become immortal, for] you . . . everything."[70]

Mary said, "There is only one saying I shall [speak] to the Master, about the mystery of truth. In this we stand and in this we appear to those who are worldly."

Judas said to Matthew, "We want to understand what sort of garments we are to be clothed with when we leave the corruption of the [flesh]."

The Master said, "The rulers and the administrators[71] have garments that are given only for a while and do not last. But you, as children of truth, are not to clothe yourselves with these garments that last only for a while. Rather, I say to you, you will be blessed when you strip off your clothing. For it is no great thing [144] [to lay aside what is] external."[72]

. . .[73] said, "Do I speak and do I receive . . . ?"

The Master said, "Yes, [one who receives] your Father in [a reflective way]."[74]

Mary Questions the Master About the Mustard Seed, and Judas Asks About Prayer

Mary asked, "[Of what] kind is the mustard seed?[75] Is it from heaven or from earth?"

The Master said, "When the Father established the world for himself, he left many things with the Mother of all.[76] That is why he sows and works."[77]

Judas said, "You have told us this from the mind of truth. When we pray, how should we pray?"

The Master said, "Pray in the place where there is no woman."

Matthew says, "He tells us, Pray in the place where there is no woman, which means, destroy the works of the female,[78] not because there is another form of birth[79] but because they should stop [giving birth]."

Mary said, "Will they never be destroyed?"

The Master said, "[You] know they will perish [once again], [145] and [the works] of [the female here] will be [destroyed as well]."[80]

Judas said [to Matthew], "The works of the [female] will perish. [Then] the rulers will [call upon their realms], and we shall be ready for them."

The Master said, "Will they see [you and will they] see those who receive you? Look, a true word[81] is coming from the Father to the abyss, silently, with a flash of lightning, and it is productive.[82] Do they see it or overcome it? No, you know more fully [the way] that [neither angel] nor authority [knows]. It is the way of the Father and the Son, for the two are one. And you will travel the [way] you have come to know. Even if the rulers become great, they will not be able to reach it. I tell you the [truth], it is even difficult for me to reach it."[83] [146]

[Mary] asked [the Master], "If the works [are destroyed, what actually] destroys a work?"

[The Master said], "You know that [when] I destroy [it, people] will go to their own places."

Judas said, "How is the spirit disclosed?"

The Master said, "How [is] the sword [disclosed]?"

Judas said, "How is the light disclosed?"

The Master said, "[It is disclosed] through itself eternally."

Judas asked, "Who forgives whose works? Do the works [forgive] the world or does the world forgive the works?"

The Master [answered], "Who [knows]? For it is the responsibility of whoever has come to know the works to do the [will] of the Father.

Conclusion

"As for you, work hard to rid yourselves of [anger] and jealousy, and strip yourselves of your [works], and do not [147] . . . . . .[84] reproach . . . . For I say to [you], . . . you receive . . . many . . . one who has sought, having [found true life]. This person will [attain rest and] live forever. I say to [you, watch yourselves], so that you may not lead [your] spirits and your souls into error."[85]

[The Dialogue] of the Savior

CHAPTER FOUR

—————

The Follower Without a Name in the
Concept of Our Great Power

THE FOURTH TRACTATE of CODEX VI of the NAG HAMMADI library is a text entitled the *Concept of Our Great Power*. The date of composition of the text is unknown, though a fourth-century date has been suggested for the document in its current form, with the likelihood that portions may have been written earlier, perhaps already in the second century. The *Concept of Our Great Power* presents an apocalyptic account of salvation history, and within the text the highest God, called the great Power, narrates the story of how people of spirit and knowledge have coped during the great ages in the history of humankind. The designation of the highest God as the "great Power" is known from other sources, including texts that discuss the first-century Samaritan teacher of gnosis Simon Magus, who went about with his companion Helena and proclaimed that he was the manifestation of the divine great Power (cf. *Acts* 8:9–25).

The *Concept of Our Great Power* opens with the great Power urging the readers of the text to explore the realities of history and human nature in order to come to an understanding of the present situation in the world and embrace a vision of hope for the future:

> *Come to know how what has gone has come to be, that you may know <how> what is alive <will> come to be. And know how to recognize this, and what that aeon looks like, what its nature is, and how it came into being.*
>
> *[Why] don't you ask what your [nature] will be, or how you have come into being? (36–37)*

The great Power then portrays human history as passing through a series of ages, and two aeons are indicated as having taken place, along with another period of time in the future: (1) the age of flesh, extending from creation through the great flood, during which time the "father of the flesh," the creator God of the Jewish Scriptures, acts in judgment; (2) the age of soul, extending from the time of the flood to the present, during which time the revealer, a man who knows the great Power, appears and does mighty things, but is persecuted by the rulers of this world; and (3) the age of spirit, which is a period of beauty yet to come, during which time the souls will be liberated and the destinies of people of knowledge will be resolved.

Jesus is not mentioned by name in the *Concept of Our Great Power*, nor is Judas Iscariot, but both are alluded to in the description of events in the age of soul. The revealer clearly is thought to be

Jesus, who is said to be a man, devoted to the great Power, who speaks in parables and proclaims the age to come, but who is opposed by the rulers of the present age, so that he descends to the realm of death, only to ascend to life once again. As a part of the account of the career of the revealer, the text describes how one of his followers—meaning Judas—hands him over to the rulers, the archons of the world (41). As in the New Testament gospels and the *Gospel of Judas,* a form of the Greek verb *paradidonai* is used in the *Concept of Our Great Power* to depict the nature of the act of this follower of Jesus, and the statement that "a fire burned in that person's soul" is similar to the lines about the passion of Judas near the end of the *Gospel of Judas* (56), especially the clause in which Jesus tells Judas, "Your anger has flared up."

The implication of the brief reference to this follower of Jesus in the *Concept of Our Great Power* is that Jesus went unrecognized in the world, until the follower handed him over and thus identified him. Judas, though unnamed, is said to be known by the rulers (the archons), and the rulers of the age discussed in the text are the lackeys of the creator God, who is the father of the flesh. Thus, it is intimated, the powers that be, including the demonic powers allied with the ruler of the underworld, use the person of Judas—or collaborate with him—in order to accomplish their nefarious deeds. These powers, the text concludes, bring judgment upon themselves. The *Concept of Our Great Power* does not specifically include Judas among those who bring condemnation down upon themselves, and the text does not necessarily accuse him of personal wrongdoing. As we shall see, however, other texts are happy to describe in detail the horrific ways in which Judas is condemned and punished for what he does.

The *Concept of Our Great Power* is a challenging document to read and comprehend, and the narrative is replete with difficult phrases, vague formulations, and terse expressions. Judas is by no means a major player in the *Concept of Our Great Power*, but as an unnamed follower of Jesus in the text he is made to act on behalf of the cosmic powers in their efforts—futile efforts, as it turns out—to oppose the mission of the revealer in this world.

THE CONCEPT OF OUR GREAT POWER[1]

Intellectual Perception
The Concept of the[2] Great Power

Whoever Knows the Great Power Will Be Saved

Whoever knows our great Power[3] will become invisible. Fire will be unable to consume such a person, but it will purify. And it will destroy all that you possess.

For all those in whom my[4] form appears, from seven days old to one hundred twenty years old,[5] will be saved.[6] Upon them are placed these obligations, to gather together all that is lost and the letters[7] of our great Power, that the great Power may write your name in our bright light and bring the thoughts and deeds of others to an end. Then these may be purified, scattered, destroyed, and brought together in the place no one can see.

You will see me and prepare your dwelling places in our great Power.

Come to know how what has gone has come to be, that you may know <how> what is alive <will> come to be. And know how to recognize this, and what that aeon looks like, [37] what its nature is, and how it came into being.

[Why] don't you ask what your [nature] will be, or how you have come into being?

In the Beginning Are Water and Spirit

Think about how immense this water is, that it is incomprehensibly immeasurable. It has no beginning; it has no end. It supports the earth and blows into the air where the gods and angels are. There is fear and light in the one exalted over all this, and my letters are visible in that one.[8]

I have provided them as a service for the creation of the flesh. For no one can stand without that one, and the aeon cannot live without that one.

That one has what is within, and thinks in a pure way.

Look at the Spirit and understand where it[9] is from.

The Spirit was given to people so that they may receive life from it day by day.

It has life within and gives to all.

Then darkness and the underworld received the fire.

It[10] will release from itself what is mine.

Its eyes could not endure my light.

The First Age, the Age of Flesh, Begins

The winds and waters moved. [38] The rest also came into being, along with the entire aeon of creation.

91

From the depths came the fire.

Power came to be in the midst of the powers.

The powers desired to see my image.

The soul became a copy of it.

This is what came into being. Notice what it is like, that before coming into being it could not be seen.[11]

Since the aeon of the flesh came to be in giant bodies, long periods of time in creation were assigned to them.[12]

When they became corrupt after entering the flesh, the father of the flesh,[13] the water, acted in judgment.

When the father of the flesh, who holds the angels in subjection, found Noah, who was pious and worthy, Noah proclaimed a message of piety for one hundred twenty years, but no one listened to him. So he made a wooden ark, and whoever he found went in. Then the flood came, [39] and Noah and his sons were saved.[14]

If there had been no ark for a person to enter, the flood water would not have come.

Thus that one had a thought and planned to save the gods, the angels, the powers, and the majesty of all of them, and the luxurious way of life, by moving them out of that aeon and providing a life for them in places that endure.

The judgment of the flesh[15] came to an end. Only the work of Power remained steadfast.

The Second Age, the Age of the Soul, Follows

Next is the aeon of the soul. It is trivial, entangled with bodies and the conception of souls and defilements. The first defilement of creation gained strength.

It produced all sorts of things—many works of wrath, anger, envy, jealousy, hatred, slander, contempt, and warfare, lies and evil advice, sorrows and pleasures, disgraces and defilements, deceits and diseases, and unjust judgments given arbitrarily.

Still you sleep [40] and dream dreams. Wake up, come back, taste and eat the food of truth.

Make the word and the water of life available.[16]

Avoid evil lusts and desires and whatever deviates from who you are.[17] These are evil dispositions that are unsound.

The mother of the fire did not have Power. She sent fire upon the soul and the land, and she burned all the dwellings in it, until her consuming rage[18] ceased. When she can find nothing else to burn, she will consume herself.

The fire will become incorporeal, with no body, and it will burn matter until it has purified everything, including all that is wicked. When it can find nothing else to burn, it will turn on itself until it consumes itself.[19]

The Revealer Comes into the World, and a Follower Hands Him Over

Then in this aeon of the soul will come the human who knows the great Power.[20] He will receive it and know me. He will drink from the milk of the mother of the work that was done. He will speak in parables and proclaim the aeon that is to come, [41] just as he spoke in the first aeon of the flesh to[21] Noah. When he uttered his words, he spoke in seventy-two languages.[22] He opened the gates of the heavens with his words. He put the ruler of the underworld[23] to shame, he raised the dead, and he destroyed the dominion of the ruler of the underworld.[24]

Then there was a great disturbance. The rulers rose up in wrath against him, and they wanted to give him over to the ruler of the underworld.

They knew one of his followers,[25] and a fire burned in that person's soul.[26] He handed him over,[27] since no one knew who he was.

They did it, they seized him, but they brought judgment upon themselves. They handed him over[28] to the ruler of the underworld.[29] They gave him over to Sasabek and Berotth.[30]

He prepared himself to go down and prove them wrong.

The Revealer Triumphs over the Archons and Ascends

Then the ruler of the underworld took him, [42] but he discovered that his flesh was such that it could not be seized and shown to the archons. He kept saying, "Who is this? What is this?"[31]

His word[32] has abolished the law of the aeon.[33]

He is from the word of the Power of life. He was stronger than the command of the rulers, and they could not dominate him by their action.

The rulers searched to find out what had happened. They did not know that this was the sign of their demise and the moment of change of the aeon.

The sun went under during the day, and the day became dark.[34] The demons were shaken.

After this he will appear as he is ascending.

The sign of the aeon that is to come will become visible, and the aeons will be dissolved.

Blessed will they be who understand what is discussed with them and will be revealed to them. Blessed will they be, for they will come to understand truth: you have found rest in the heavens.

Many Follow the Revealer and
Record His Words

Then many will follow him, and they will labor in the regions where they were born. [43]

They will go about and write down his words as they wish.[35]

Observe that these aeons are gone. How large is the water of the aeon that has dissolved? What are the dimensions of aeons? How will people prepare themselves, how will they be established, how will they become indestructible aeons?

At first, after his preaching, he proclaims the second aeon, along with the first.

The first aeon must perish with the passing of time.

He spent time in the first aeon, as he went about in it until it perished, and he preached for one hundred twenty years.[36] This is the perfect number, which is held in high regard.[37]

He made the border of the west desolate, and he destroyed the east.

Your seed and those who wish to follow our great word[38] and his proclamation <...>.

The Archons Attack the Place Where
the Word First Appeared

Then the wrath of the rulers burned. They were ashamed of their dissolution.

They fumed and grew angry at life. Cities were overthrown; mountains dissolved.

The ruler came, with the [44] rulers of the west, to the east, to the place where the word first appeared.[39]

Then the earth trembled and the cities were shaken.[40]

The birds ate and had their fill of their dead.[41]

The earth mourned, along with the inhabited world. They were desolate.

When the times were completed, wickedness increased greatly, until the final end of the word.

Then the ruler of the west arose.[42] He will act from the east and will teach people his wickedness. He wishes to eradicate all teaching of words of true wisdom,[43] for he loves false wisdom.[44]

He raised his hand against what is old, with the intent of bringing wickedness in and dressing in the clothing of dignity. He could not do it, because his garments are exceptionally filthy.

Then he got angry and made an appearance. He wished to go up and pass over to that place.

The moment came, and he approached. He changes the ordinances.

The Imitator Reigns over the Earth and Leads People Astray

Then the time came when the child grew up. When he reached maturity, [45] the rulers sent the imitator[45] to that person,[46] so that they might come to know our great Power. They expected that he would work a sign for them, and he performed great signs.[47]

He[48] reigned over the whole earth and all who are under heaven. He set his throne over the end of the earth.

It is said, "I shall make you God of the world."

He will perform signs and wonders.

The people will turn from me and go astray.

Those people who follow the imitator will introduce circumcision. He will pronounce judgment upon those who are from the uncircumcision, who are the real people.

For he has sent many preachers beforehand, and they have preached on his behalf.

Souls Are Purified as Apocalyptic Signs Appear

When he has completed the time set for the kingdom of the earth, the purification of souls will occur, for wickedness has become stronger than you.

The powers will tremble. All the seas will dry up. The firmament will not send down dew.

The springs will stop giving water. The rivers will no longer flow [46] back to their springs. The waters of the springs of the earth will stop flowing.[49]

The depths will be laid bare and will lie open.

The stars will expand and the sun will stop shining.[50]

I shall withdraw with all those who know me.

They will enter into immeasurable light, where there is no being of flesh or seduction of fire to seize them. They will be free and holy, and no one will be able to drag them down. I am protecting them with my hand, and they have holy garments that fire cannot touch.

Next are darkness, wind, and a moment as short as the blink of an eye.

Then he will come to destroy everything.

They will be chastised until they are pure.

The period of time allotted for them to have power is 1468 years.[51]

When the fire has consumed everything and can find nothing else to burn, it will extinguish itself.[52]

Then the [47] [judgment of fire], which is the [second] power, will be completed.

The Third Age, the Age of the Spirit, Is an Aeon of Beauty

Then mercy will come . . . through Sophia . . . .

The firmaments [will collapse] down to the abyss.

The children of matter will perish. From that moment they will not exist.

Then will appear the souls who are holy through the light of the Power that is exalted above all powers, the immeasurable, the universal. That is I, and all who know me.

They will be in the aeon of beauty, of the aeon of marriage,[53] and they will be adorned through Sophia.

After praising the one who is in incomprehensible oneness, they behold him[54] on account of his[55] will that is within them.

They all have come to be as reflections in his light. They all have shone, and they have found rest in his rest.

The one who is in oneness will free the souls being chastised, and they come to live in purity.

They will see the holy ones and call out to them, "Have mercy on us, Power above all powers."[56] For [48] . . . in the iniquity that exists . . . to him their eyes.

[They] do not seek him because they do not seek us, nor do they believe us. They have acted in accordance with the creation of the rulers and the other rulers of creation. We also have behaved according to our fleshly origin, in the creation of the rulers, which establishes law.

Yet we are the ones who have come to live in the unchangeable aeon.[57]

The Concept of Our Great Power

CHAPTER FIVE

The Traitor in the "Round Dance of the Cross"

THE "ROUND DANCE OF THE CROSS," OR "HYMN OF JESUS," is a song included within the *Acts of John*, and it is said that Jesus taught this song and the accompanying dance to his disciples before he was handed over to be crucified. This lovely, mystical hymn has been used in literature and film, and Gustav Holst set it to music in *The Hymn of Jesus*. In the "Round Dance of the Cross," Jesus sings the verses of the hymn, and the disciples respond, antiphonally, by singing "Amen" as they dance in a circle around Jesus. The verses Jesus sings consist largely of aretalogical self-predications—"I am" statements—which are frequently riddlelike and paradoxical in character. The textual history of the *Acts of John* and the "Round Dance of the Cross" within it is complicated, but it is often assumed that the *Acts of John* was composed in Syria in the latter part of the second century or a bit later. The "Round Dance of the Cross" seems to employ themes derived from the Johannine tradition, and it may reflect the Gnostic concerns of the mystical followers of the great teacher Valentinus.

Although Judas Iscariot is not referred to by name in the "Round Dance of the Cross," two passages are of interest for our examination of Judas traditions. In the introduction to the hymn, which contains comments that disparage both the Jewish people and the Jewish God as being lawless and describe their God as the serpent, Jesus invites the disciples to join him in song before he is handed over to the Jews. After singing together, Jesus says, they will be able to go out to face what is to take place—namely, the events surrounding the delivering up of Jesus to his death. Near the conclusion of the hymn, Jesus declares to the disciples that he is their God but not the God of the traitor. Although the reference to the traitor is somewhat ambiguous, it seems to designate Judas as the traitor, who is no longer associated with the divine Christ but who stands condemned, estranged from God.

THE ROUND DANCE OF THE CROSS[1]

[94] Before he (Jesus) was apprehended by the lawless Jews, who have received their law from the lawless serpent,[2] he gathered all of us together and said, "Before I am handed over to them,[3] let's sing a hymn to the Father and hence go to face what lies ahead."

So he told us to form a circle and hold each other's hands, and he stood in the middle and said, "Respond to me with 'Amen.'"

The Song

He began singing a hymn and declaring,

> Glory to you, Father.

We circled around him and responded,

> Amen.

> Glory to you, Word.[4]
> Glory to you, Grace.
>   Amen.

> Glory to you, Spirit.
> Glory to you, Holy One.
> Glory to your glory.
>   Amen.

> We praise you, Father.
> We thank you, light,
> in whom no darkness lives.[5]
>   Amen.

> [95] I declare why we offer thanks:
> I will[6] be saved and I will save.
>   Amen.

I will be released and I will release.
　Amen.

I will be wounded and I will wound.
　Amen.

I will be born and I will bear.
　Amen.

I will eat and I will be eaten.
　Amen.

I will hear and I will be heard.
　Amen.

I will be in mind, I, pure mind.
　Amen.

I will be washed and I will wash.
　Amen.

Grace dances.[7]

I will play the flute.
Dance, everyone.
　Amen.

I will weep.
Lament, everyone.
　Amen.

A realm of eight[8] sings with us.
　Amen.

The twelfth number[9] dances above.
   Amen.

The whole universe joins in dancing.
   Amen.

If you do not dance you do not know what is.
   Amen.

I will run away and I will remain.
   Amen.

I will adorn and I will be adorned.
   Amen.

I will be united and I will unite.
   Amen.

I am homeless and I have homes.
   Amen.

I have no place and I have places.
   Amen.

I have no temple and I have temples.
   Amen.

I am a lamp to you who see me.
   Amen.

I am a mirror to you who recognize me.
   Amen.

I am a door[10] *to you who knock on me.*
    Amen.

I am a way[11] *to you, passerby.*[12]
    Amen.

Understanding the Song

[96] *If you follow my dance,*
see yourself in me when I speak.
If you have seen what I do,
keep quiet about my mysteries.

You who dance, consider what I do.
Yours is the human passion I am to suffer.
You could never understand what you suffer
unless I, the word, was sent to you by the Father.

You who have seen what I do
have seen me as suffering,
and when you saw it,
you did not stand still
but were utterly moved.
You were moved to wisdom,
and you have my help.

Rest in me.

Who I am
you will know when I go.
What I am seen to be now
I am not.

What I am
you will see when you come.

If you knew how to suffer
you would be able not to suffer.
Learn how to suffer
and you will be able not to suffer.

What you do not know
I shall teach you.
I am your God,
not the traitor's.[13]
I wish holy souls
to be in harmony with me.
Know the word of wisdom.

Say again with me,

Glory to you, Father.
Glory to you, Word.
Glory to you, Spirit.
    Amen.

If you wish to know what I was,
I ridiculed everything with the word,[14]
and I was not ridiculed[15] *at all.*[16]
I jumped for joy.
Understand everything,
and when you have understood, declare,
Glory to you, Father.
    Amen.

CHAPTER SIX

Judas the Diabolical
in Other Christian Texts

FROM THE SECOND CENTURY ON, THE FIGURE OF JUDAS ISCARIOT has been increasingly demonized in much of Christian literature, and more often than not he has been portrayed, in Christian literature and art, as the stereotypical bad Jew. In this way the character of Judas Iscariot has served as a vehicle for the expression of hostility and contempt, particularly against Jewish people, and Judas has played an important role, though in caricature, in the development and expression of anti-Semitic sentiments. In this chapter I present a few of the texts, from Papias through Sedulius to the *Golden Legend* and beyond, that expand the story of Judas and suggest that Judas, from youth to eternal punishment, was the personification of all that is evil. I make no pretenses that this is a complete presentation of texts, and I refer readers to the research of Bart Ehrman and Kim Paffenroth and to additional portrayals of Judas in the apostolic fathers, the *Acts of Peter,* the *Acts of Thomas,* other Bartholomew materials, and the church fathers Jerome, Ambrose, and John Chrysostom. Here I offer representative selections from ten texts that give a vivid picture of some of the imaginative ways—almost exclusively negative—in which the Judas legend developed through the centuries.

The texts in this chapter are arranged in such a manner as to allow for a general narrative flow from an account of Judas as a naughty boy who takes it out on Jesus to texts that depict the final fate of Judas in hell and interpret him as someone walking in the footsteps of Oedipus. This arrangement does not reflect the precise chronological order of the texts, and note should be taken of the approximate dates of composition of the texts given here. The earliest of the selections about Judas the diabolical is most likely the fragment from Papias, bishop of Hierapolis in Asia Minor (present-day Turkey), who wrote a five-volume work entitled *Expositions of the Sayings of the Lord* sometime in the first half of the second century. The passage translated here is from Book 4 of his long work, and this fragment is preserved in the writings of Apollinaris of Laodicea, who did his literary work in the fourth century.

One of the latest—though perhaps not the very latest—of the selections must be the text from the *Golden Legend,* or *Legenda Aurea,* which was composed by a Dominican monk named Jacobus de Voragine (or Jacob of Virragio), in the thirteenth century, between 1260 and 1275. Later he became archbishop of Genoa. In the *Golden Legend,* Jacobus de Voragine compiled traditions about the disciples of Jesus and Christian saints, and his work became a bestseller. In Chapter 45 he retells the story of Judas (in part an apocryphal story, he says) with themes derived from the New Testament and early Christian traditions as well as from the legendary life of King Oedipus of Thebes, the tragic figure featured in the famous dramatic production of the Greek playwright Sophocles, who kills his father and marries his mother. In the *Golden Legend* the story of Oedipus is adapted to Judas Iscariot, who is described acting similarly toward his father and mother. In this text Judas is so guilt-stricken by what he has done to his parents that he goes to Jesus to be forgiven of his sins—and then he betrays Jesus for thirty coins.

Between the second and thirteenth centuries, and even after that, other texts were written about Judas Iscariot. The dating of ancient and late antique texts is hardly an exact science, but there is some agreement among scholars that the text called the *Gospel of Nicodemus*, or the *Acts of Pilate*, may be assigned a date around the later half of the fourth century. Furthermore, we know that the Christian author Sedulius wrote his influential *Paschal Hymn*, or *Carmen Paschale*, in the early part of the fifth century as a gospel epic in imitation of classical epic poetry, such as that of Virgil. Except for Papias, the other texts presented in this chapter can hardly have been composed much earlier, and in some cases the date of composition may be quite a bit later than the fourth or fifth century.

Probably the most recently written text included here is the *Gospel of Barnabas*. Although it is sometimes suggested that this gospel may have incorporated older material and some readers are inclined to favor a rather early date for the text, most scholars assign a very late date of composition, perhaps as late as the sixteenth century. The *Gospel of Barnabas* maintains that it was not Jesus who was crucified but rather Judas, who was made to resemble Jesus and was mistaken for him by the soldiers who did the crucifying. Such a gospel message may help to interpret a passage in the Qur'an, Surah 4, where it is said that Jesus ('Isa in Arabic) was not actually executed:

> They said (in boast),
> "We killed Christ Jesus
> the son of Mary,
> the messenger of Allah"—
> but they killed him not,
> nor crucified him,
> but so it was made
> to appear to them,
> and those who differ
> therein are full of doubts,
> with no (certain) knowledge,
> but only conjecture to follow,
> for of a surety
> they killed him not—
> no, Allah raised him up
> unto himself; and Allah
> is exalted in power, wise.[1]

The Qur'an, in turn, reflects in part a similar claim to be found in traditions, particularly Gnostic traditions in the Nag Hammadi *Revelation of Peter* and *Second Discourse of Great Seth* and the teachings of Basilides (according to Irenaeus of Lyon), that the true person of Christ did not die on the cross, but that some substitute was crucified in his place—perhaps the physical, biological body of Christ or perhaps, according to Basilides, Simon of Cyrene—while the real, spiritual Jesus stood by laughing at the ignorance of those who thought they could kill him. This position may also be compared with intimations in the *Gospel of Judas* about the true, spiritual person of Jesus and the impending arrest, in which Judas himself will be involved.

Taken together, in narrative sequence, these selections on Judas give us glimpses of moments in the development of Judas legends. He is, it is maintained in the *Arabic Infancy Gospel,* a bad boy from his youth, and he literally is filled with the devil. When he hits young Jesus on the side, it is said to be the very spot where one day the Jews will pierce Jesus with a spear. This recalls the account of the piercing of the side of Jesus in *John* 19:34, except that a soldier does the piercing in the *Gospel of John* and the Jews are blamed for it in the *Infancy Gospel.*

As an adult, Judas is described by Papias as being utterly repulsive, and in the *Narrative of Joseph of Arimathea* he is paid to be a stool pigeon in the circle of the disciples. (In another fragment of a Christian text, not translated here, Judas is said to have remained apart from the rest of the disciples on the occasion of the miraculous feeding of the multitude, and so he does not receive any of the bread to pass around to the people. In Christian interpretation, the bread is commonly understood in a eucharistic fashion to represent the body of Christ, and Judas, unworthy as he is, does not touch it.) The Christian poet Sedulius, sometimes dubbed "the Christian Virgil," heaps poetic abuse upon Judas, and his account of Judas is a veritable thesaurus of negative epithets and descriptive phrases. In textual fragments associated with the apostolic name of Bartholomew, Judas's wife is described as a bad influence upon him, and the *Gospel of Nicodemus* (or *Acts of Pilate*) tells a tale of a half-baked rooster that crows and convinces Judas that he had better go out and hang himself. Jesus gives Judas a second chance after the betrayal in the *Acts of Andrew and Paul*, but Judas goes out to the desert and, in fear, bows down and worships the devil.

As noted, Judas is crucified instead of Jesus in the *Gospel of Barnabas*, and he finally is turned over to be punished in hell. In the *Book of the Resurrection of Christ by Bartholomew the Apostle*, Judas is accused by Jesus of handing him over to "the Jewish dogs," and the torments he will endure in hell are enumerated in fiendish detail. As in Dante's *Inferno*, Judas is subjected to some of the worst punishments imaginable. Dante visualizes Judas down in the ninth and lowest circle of hell—the circle of treachery—with Brutus and Cassius, the assassins of Julius Caesar, where all three are gnawed on forever by the three mouths of Lucifer. In Dante, it is Judas's head that is inside the middle mouth of Lucifer, who also claws at Judas's back and rips it open. Thus Judas Iscariot, the wicked and diabolical betrayer of Christ, takes his place among the worst of the damned in hell, according to Dante and the *Book of the Resurrection of Christ*—until the time that readers might reexamine and reinterpret the early accounts of the life of Judas, the sands of Egypt might yield a papyrus copy of the long lost *Gospel of Judas*, and the figure of Judas Iscariot might at last, perhaps, be redeemed.

The Boy Judas, Filled with the Devil, Bullies Young Jesus

Arabic Infancy Gospel 35[2]

Another woman was living there, and her son was tormented by Satan. This boy was named Judas, and whenever Satan seized him, he would bite whoever came near him, and if he found no one around him, he would bite his own hands and his other limbs. The mother of this miserable lad heard about the fame of Lady Mary and her son Jesus, and so she got up and brought her son Judas with her to Lady Mary.

Meanwhile, James and Joses[3] had taken the child, the Lord Jesus, to play with the other children, and they left the house and sat down, and the Lord Jesus with them. Demon-possessed Judas came by and sat to the right of Jesus. Then he was attacked by Satan in the same way as usually happened, and he wanted to bite the Lord Jesus, but he couldn't. Nevertheless, he hit Jesus on the right side, and as a result Jesus began to cry. Immediately Satan departed from that boy and fled like a mad dog.

Now, this boy who hit Jesus and from whom Satan departed in the form of a dog was Judas Iscariot, who handed him over to the Jews. And the same side on which Judas hit him is where the Jews pierced him with a spear.[4]

Judas Is Repulsive in Both Character and Appearance

Papias, Expositions of the Sayings of the Lord, Book 4, fragment 4[5]

Judas went around in this world as a supreme example of impiety. He grew to be so bloated in his flesh that he could not squeeze through an opening a chariot could easily go through—not even his bulging head. They say that his eyelids got so swollen that he could not see any light, and a doctor could not observe his eyes, even with an optical instrument, because they were buried so deep in the surrounding tissue. His genitals became more massive and repulsive than anyone else's, and when he relieved himself, to his perverse shame, he discharged the pus and worms that streamed all through his body. They say that after suffering many torments and punishments, he died on his own piece of property, and that property has become, to the present day, desolate and uninhabited on account of the putrid smell. In fact, to this day no one can pass by that place without plugging his nose with his hands. This is how great the flow of fluid from his flesh was onto the ground.[6]

Judas: A Phony Follower Who Accuses Jesus of Stealing the Law

Narrative of Joseph of Arimathea, or a Pilate text, 1–2[7]

(1) I am Joseph of Arimathea. I requested the body of the Lord Jesus from Pilate, in order to bury it, and for this reason I was confined in prison by the Jews, who murder and fight against God. While observing the law, they also have become through Moses himself agents of tribulation. For they made the lawgiver angry; without recognizing him, they crucified God, and they made it manifest to those who knew that the Son of God was crucified.

Seven days before Christ endured his passion, two condemned criminals were sent from Jericho to the procurator Pilate. This is the case against them.

The first, named Gestas,[8] killed travelers on the road, murdering them with the sword, and he stripped others and left them naked. He strung up women by their heels, with their heads down, and he cut off their breasts; and he engaged in the drinking of blood from the limbs of babies. He never knew God and did not obey his laws, but he was violent, and from the beginning he did these sorts of deeds.

The case against the other one was like this. He was called Demas[9] and was a Galilean by birth, and he ran an inn. He attacked the rich but treated the poor well. He was a thief like Tobit, for he buried the corpses of the poor.[10] He turned his attention to robbing the Jewish multitude, and he stole the law itself in Jerusalem, stripped the clothing off Caiaphas's daughter, who was the priestess of the sanctuary, and took away that secret deposit left there by Solomon. This is what his deeds were like.

Jesus also was taken into custody on the third day before Passover, when it was nighttime. But for Caiaphas and the Jewish multitude it was no Passover, but rather it was a time of great mourning, because of the plundering of the sanctuary by the thief.

They called in Judas Iscariot and spoke with him, for he was the son of the brother of Caiaphas the priest. He was not personally a disciple of Jesus, but the whole Jewish multitude urged him, in an underhanded way, to follow Jesus, not that he might be obedient to the signs done by him or confess him, but that he might catch him saying something false and hand him over to them. They gave him gifts for such audacity, together with two drachmai a day.[11] For two years he acted like this in the company of Jesus, as one of his disciples called John says.

On the third day,[12] before Jesus was taken into custody, Judas said to the Jews, "Come, let's convene a council, for maybe it was not the thief who stole the law, but rather Jesus himself. This is the accusation I bring against him."

When these words had been spoken, Nicodemus, who kept the keys to the sanctuary, came in with us, and he said to everyone, "Don't do anything of the sort." For Nicodemus was more honest than the entire Jewish multitude.

Then the daughter of Caiaphas, named Sarah, called out and said, "Well, he himself spoke, in the presence of all, against this holy place: 'I can destroy this Temple and raise it in three days.'"[13]

The Jews said to her, "You are more trustworthy than any of us." For they considered her to be a prophetess. And, to be sure, after the council had met, Jesus was taken into custody.

(2) The next day, which was the fourth day of the week,[14] they led him at the ninth hour[15] into Caiaphas's hall. Annas and Caiaphas said to him, "Tell us, why have you stolen our law and renounced what was declared in Moses and the prophets?"

Jesus gave no answer.

Again, a second time, while the multitude was present, they said to him, "Why do you want to destroy in one moment the sanctuary that it took Solomon forty-six years to build?"

Jesus gave no answer to these things. For the sanctuary of the place of assembly[16] had been plundered by the thief.

When the evening of the fourth day came to a close, the whole Jewish multitude sought to burn Caiaphas's daughter because of the loss of the law, for they did not know how they were going to observe Passover.

And she said to them, "Wait a minute, my children. Let's destroy this fellow Jesus, and the law will be found and the holy festival will be celebrated fully and completely."

Secretly Annas and Caiaphas gave a goodly amount of money to Judas Iscariot, and said, "Repeat what you previously said to us—'I know that the law was stolen by Jesus'—so that the accusation may be made against him and not against this young girl, who is blameless."

When Judas received these instructions, he said to them, "Don't let the whole multitude know that I have been coached by you to do this against Jesus. But let Jesus go, and I'll persuade the multitude that this is so."

In a devious way they let Jesus go.

Judas went into the sanctuary at daybreak on the fifth day,[17] and he said to all the people, "What are you willing to give me for me to hand over to you the one who has overthrown the law and has pillaged the prophets?"

The Jews said to him, "If you hand him over to us, we shall give you thirty gold coins."[18] The people did not know that Judas was speaking about Jesus, for a substantial number of them confessed that he was the Son of God. Then Judas received the thirty gold coins.

He was going out at the fourth hour,[19] and the fifth,[20] and he found Jesus walking on the street. When evening was approaching, Judas said to the Jews, "Help me out with soldiers armed with swords and clubs, and I shall hand him over to you."

So they gave him officers for the purpose of arresting him.

As they were on the way, Judas says to them, "Arrest the one I shall kiss, for it is he who has stolen the law and the prophets."

So, he went up to Jesus and kissed him, and said, "Hello, Rabbi." It was the evening of the fifth day.[21]

They seized him and handed him over to Caiaphas and the high priests, and Judas said, "This is the one who has stolen the law and the prophets."

The Jews held an unjust trial for Jesus, and they said, "Why did you do this?"

He gave no answer.

When Nicodemus and I, Joseph, saw the seat of the plagues, we stood apart from them, for we did not want to perish in the counsel of the godless.[22]

Judas: A Cruel Betrayer, Vicious Traitor, and Merciless Thief

Sedulius, Paschal Hymn 5.20–68 [23]

Then, celebrating the paschal feast as usual
by the observance of a sacred meal, Christ makes himself
the humble servant, setting a fitting example for his disciples;
he gets up, wearing a linen cloth, and gladly
serves his servants, extending them great honor.
In this way he washes the feet of each disciple freely,
in order to expose Judas, whom he knows to be the author
of unrighteous treachery.[24] But that honor was nothing to you,
savage traitor——it was reserved for cleaner feet!
Your heart was fouled, just as every tomb
is covered with a veil of white on the outside,
but within, a shroud is filled with a putrid corpse.[25]
His lies were not unknown to the Lord, who revealed
the author of that future sin by handing bread to him——
he who was himself the bread about to be handed over;
for, he later sanctified the two gifts of his body and blood,
and gave both food and drink, through which without fail
our faithful souls might never thirst or hunger.

All of a sudden a filthy spirit entered Judas
where envy had its seat, and taking arms against the Lord,
it made him rouse a servant's war,
and he agreed to do great evil for whatever the reward.
Blame is not put on him for the price, though, but the cost.
Blinded by a small reward, he takes thirty coins of silver,[26]
but was about to take in as much sin, as if he had stolen
all the kingdoms of the earth at once, the riches of the sea
and all of the heavens along with the wandering clouds.
All the wealth in the world could not account
for the bloodshed of almighty Christ, who is
the Father of the world, who made it and gave it life.

O would that he had been damned to a sterile womb
and never known his day of birth,
nor drawn the pleasing airs of life with vital breath,
but stayed hidden in eternal sleep; it would have been better,
that he had never known life rather than waste the one he was given;
or better still, that he had lost his gifts of life from the start,
being cast to the ground just as dust is blown from the
face of the earth by driving gales and great wind,
scattered into the empty shadows and obscured by cloud.

You bloody, savage, rash, insane, rebellious,
faithless, cruel, deceitful, bribable, unjust,
cruel betrayer, vicious traitor, merciless thief—
are you the standard-bearer for these fearsome swords?
Do you command the sacrilegious ranks that threaten us
with point and spear, as you press your face to his and mix your

poison with his honey, and betray the Lord under the pretense of
affection?
Why do you pretend to be his ally and greet him with loving treachery?
Peace never conspires with terrible swords,
nor does the wolf give fearsome kisses to the pious lamb.

Judas's Wife Encourages Him to Betray Jesus, and She Is Denounced by the Son of Joseph of Arimathea

Gospel of Bartholomew, or another Bartholomew
or apostolic text (fragments)[27]

Now [we] found that man (Judas) stealing from what was deposited in the money bag every day, bringing it to his wife, and diminishing what was given to the poor serving among them.[28] At times, when he went home with some of the proceeds in his hands, she expressed her pleasure with him. We also observed him when he did not bring enough to her to satisfy the evil in her eyes and her insatiable greed, and she showed her contempt for him.

In this way, then, in keeping with the insatiable greed and the evil eye of this woman, one day he was at home and she gave him advice in strong and fearful terms: "Look, the Jews are pursuing your master. Get up and hand him over to them. They will pay you a lot of money, and we shall use it for our life and our house."

The wretch got up after he heard what his wife had to say, and so he brought misery upon his soul in Tartaros in the realm of death. He followed her advice just as Adam listened to his wife, and he became estranged from the glory of paradise and death dominated him and all his offspring. This also is what happened to Judas when he listened to his wife, and he became estranged from the things of heaven and the things of earth, and he reached the realm of death, the place of weeping and groaning.

Well, then, he went to the Jews and set the price with them at thirty silver coins for him to hand over his master. They agreed and paid him.

Thus was fulfilled what was written: "They received thirty silver coins as the price of an honorable man."[29]

He got up and brought the money to his evil wife.

He said to her, . . .

When the devil entered into the apostle Judas, he left and hurried to the high priest.

He said to them, "What will you give me to hand him (Jesus) over to you?"

They gave him thirty silver coins.

Now, Judas's wife took care of the son of Joseph of Arimathea and served as his nurse.

On the very day when that miserable Judas received the thirty silver coins from the Jews and brought the money home, the child did not [want to nurse].

Joseph [went] into the room of the woman . . . Judas . . . .

Joseph went in . . . , distressed [over] his son.

When the little boy, who was seven months old, saw his father, he cried and said, "My father, come here. Take me from the hands of this monster of a woman, for at the ninth hour yesterday they received the price . . . ."

After he [heard this], his father picked [him] up.

Judas also left. He took . . . with the other people of the king. They seized Jesus and brought him to the procurator.

Judas Asks His Wife to Help Him Prepare to Hang Himself

Gospel of Nicodemus, or Acts of Pilate (manuscript reading)[30]

He (Judas) went home to make a noose of rope, in order to hang himself, and he found his wife sitting down and roasting a cock over a charcoal fire prior to eating it.

And he said to her, "Get up, wife, and find a rope for me, because I want to hang myself, as I deserve."

But his wife said to him, "Why are you saying these sorts of things?"

Judas said to her, "In truth, you should know that I have handed my teacher Jesus over in a wicked way to the evildoers, so that Pilate might execute him. But he will rise again on the third day—and woe to us!"

His wife said to him, "Don't speak or think like that. For it is just as possible for this cock roasting over the charcoal fire to crow as for Jesus to rise again, as you are saying."

And immediately, as she finished speaking, that cock spread its wings and crowed three times.[31]

Then Judas was convinced even more, and immediately he made the noose of rope and hanged himself.

Judas Repents, but Ends Up Worshiping the Devil

Acts of Andrew and Paul 119–22[32]

(119) It happened, when I (Paul) came to the underworld, that I saw the dwelling places of all the souls.[33] I saw Judas, the apostle who walked with our Lord, undergoing great and grievous torment. I said to him, "What are you doing being punished like this? Didn't the Lord take you away with all these souls that he released?"

Judas said to me, "Woe is me, doubly so, for what I have done to my Master, for I have sinned against him! I handed him over to the Jews for silver coins, which perish. To be sure, I knew that he was [my] Master and the Master of the whole earth. I went off, took [my] silver coins, and gave them back to the high priests.

"I begged him, 'My Master, forgive me. You won't abandon me, will you, on account of a single thing that I have done, since I have sold you for money? Don't abandon me. Will you watch me go down to perdition?[34] Remember me, my Master. For I heard you speaking with the apostle Peter when he asked you, "If my brother sins against me, how many times shall I forgive him? As many as seven times?" You said to him, "<Not> seven times; seven times seventy."[35] Now, as for me, I have sinned against you only once. (120) Will you watch me go down to perdition? No, my Master. What man would watch his son go down to perdition and not help him? And if I, if I dared to hand you over, will you watch me go down to perdition? No, my Master.'

"Then he sent me into the desert and said to me, 'Fear no one but God alone. If you see the devil coming, do not fear him, nor anyone except God alone.'

"Now, I went off to the mountain to fast, so that God might forgive me. The ruler of perdition approached me; he raised his head over me, and he opened his mouth and was about to devour me. I was afraid, and I worshiped him, saying, 'You are my Master.' At once he left me.

"And I, I wept, for there was no repentance left for me. I thought, What shall I do? If the Master were here, I would go and plead with him—but he had already been brought to the Praetorium to be tried. I said, I'll go and hang myself, and then I'll get to the realm of death before him.

"He descended to this place and released all these souls, as he laid waste the realm of death—except for my soul alone.

"The doorkeepers of the realm of death wept before the devil and (121) said, 'What are you doing, boasting about yourself and saying, "I am the king, and there is no one besides me"?[36] Now we understand that you are not the only king, for the one who is the Master came to you and took them all away from you.'

"Then the devil said, in the presence of all his hosts, 'O my powers, all of you, do you really think that he is mightier than we are? No. Rather, he has come here, but look, there is one other soul that he could not release.'

"Then Jesus called to Michael,[37] whom he had brought with him down to the realm of death. He said to him, 'Bring up the soul of Judas, so that the devil might not have an advantage over <me>.'

"Michael came and brought me up, and after that Michael called out, 'Shame on you, you impotent foe!'

"[Following] this, the Master said to Michael, '[Make] the soul [return] to Tartaros in the realm of death.'"

Judas wept: "Will you go off and leave me in these torments? If I once again make my soul leave the body, it is because I know you are going to the realm of death and will take away all these souls, and so you may take mine as well."

Jesus answered and said to Judas, "You wretch! What were you doing just before you bowed down and worshiped the devil?"

Judas said to him, "Master, he came upon me in the form of a dragon, and he had [his] mouth open and was about to devour me. I was afraid, and I worshiped him."

[Jesus] said to him, "O you wretch! The moment he came toward you, if you had said, 'Jesus, help me,' you would have been saved. But you offered a different form of service and you have done something God hates; you have brought death upon yourself. That is why you must stay in Tartaros until judgment day, when the Master will pass judgment on you."

"And I have been here since that day."

Judas Mistaken for Jesus and Crucified

Gospel of Barnabas 216–17 (selections) [38]

(216) In an impulsive manner, Judas went before anyone else into the room from which Jesus had been taken up. The disciples were asleep. Then the marvelous God acted marvelously, for Judas was so completely transformed in his speech and appearance to resemble Jesus that we were convinced he was Jesus.[39] He woke us up, and he asked where the Master was. We were amazed, and we replied, "Lord, you are our Master. Have you forgotten us?"

He smiled and said, "Now you are being foolish, not recognizing me as Judas Iscariot."

While he was saying this, a military force came in and seized Judas, since he resembled Jesus in every respect.

When we heard Judas's comment and saw all the soldiers, we fled in a frenzy.

John was wrapped up in linen, and he woke up and fled, and when a soldier grabbed on to him by the linen, he left the linen behind and fled naked.[40]

So God heard Jesus's prayer, and he saved the eleven from evil.

(217) The soldiers took Judas and bound him, and they mocked him. He told the truth and insisted that he was not Jesus, but the soldiers ridiculed him and said, "Your highness, do not be afraid, because we have come to make you the king of Israel. We have bound you only because we know that you refuse to receive the kingdom."

Judas answered, "You are out of your minds. You are here to take Jesus of Nazareth, with weapons and lamps, as if you are after a robber—and you have bound me, the one who has led you here, in order to make me the king."

The soldiers grew impatient and began to strike Judas with their fists and their feet, and in a rage they took him into Jerusalem.

John and Peter followed the soldiers from afar, and they told the present author that they observed the entire interrogation of Judas by the high priest and the council of the Pharisees, who had come together in order to execute Jesus. Judas spoke crazy things, so that everybody laughed heartily, since they were sure that he really was Jesus and was pretending to be crazy because he was afraid he was going to die.

So the soldiers put a blindfold over his eyes and poked fun of him and said, "Jesus, prophet of the Nazarenes"—that is what they called those who believed in Jesus—"tell us who hit you." And they beat him and spit in his face.

Now, God had decreed what would happen, and he made sure that Judas would be crucified, so that he would suffer the same terrible death to which he had sold another person. He did not let Judas die by being scourged, even though the soldiers whipped him so horribly that blood rained from his body.

Then, to mock him, they clothed him in an old purple robe and said, "Our new king should be clothed and crowned."

They brought thorns and assembled a crown like the crowns of gold and jewels that kings wear on their heads. They placed this crown on Judas's head, put a reed in his hand as a scepter, and made him sit on high. The soldiers approached him, bowed down in jest, and greeted him as the king of the Jews. They held out their hands so that he might give them gifts, as is the custom for new kings. But when they received nothing, they struck Judas and said, "Why are you crowned, foolish king, if you will not give payment to your soldiers and servants?"

The high priests, scholars, and Pharisees saw that Judas did not die from being scourged, and they were afraid that Pilate might free him. So they offered a monetary gift to the governor, and after he accepted it, he turned Judas over to the scholars and Pharisees as one who was guilty and should be executed. They in turn condemned two robbers, and him, to be crucified.

They led him to Mount Calvary, where they were in the habit of hanging evildoers, and they crucified him there, naked, to shame him even more.

Judas in truth only called out, "God, why have you forsaken me, for the evildoer has gotten away, but I am dying unjustly?"[41]

I am telling the truth, the voice, appearance, and person of Judas resembled Jesus so closely that his disciples and believers were completely convinced that he was Jesus. As a result, some forsook the doctrine of Jesus and believed that Jesus had been a false prophet, and that the miracles he had performed he had done through magic. For Jesus had said that he would not die until the end of the world, so that he would be taken out of the world at that time.

But those who were steadfast in the doctrine of Jesus were so filled with sadness at the death of one who looked just like Jesus that they forgot what Jesus had said. Along with Jesus's mother, they went to Mount Calvary, and they witnessed the death of Judas, with many tears, and obtained the body of Judas from the governor, with the help of Nicodemus and Joseph of Arimathea, so that they might bury it. Thus, they took his body down from the cross, with weeping that was beyond belief, and they buried it in Joseph's new tomb, having embalmed his body with a hundred pounds of precious unguents.

Judas Cursed with Punishments and Torments in Hell

Book of the Resurrection of Christ by Bartholomew the Apostle 3b–5a[42]

(3b) Jesus descended [into hell, and] he scattered [the demons] and bound the devil. And he redeemed Adam and all his children, and saved humanity. He had pity on his image, and liberated all of creation and all the world. He provided healing for his offspring, whom the enemy had wounded. He, the holy and faithful shepherd, brought the wayward sheep back to his fold again. And he brought Adam back to his original state again, and forgave them[43] their sins. In peace, Amen.

Then the Savior turned to the man who had handed him over, Judas Iscariot, and he said to him, "Tell me, Judas, what did you [gain] by handing me, [your Master], over to the Jewish dogs? To be sure, I [endured] all sorts of suffering in order to fulfill [the will of my] Father and redeem and [liberate my creation] that I had made. [But] you, [woe to you, with] woe that is doubled . . . .[44]

(4a) "[His (Judas's) name has been erased] from the book [of] life. His name has been removed from [the scroll] of the saints. His [inheritance] has been taken away from among the living. His writing slate has been smashed. The oil in his jar has been poured out [and wasted]. His robe has been torn. [Satan] has [taken] him [to court], and he has come forth condemned. His position as overseer has been taken out of his hands.[45] His [crown] has been seized. Strangers have snatched away in a moment what he has produced with hard work. He is blanketed with a curse as with a garment. He is poured out like water. The robe that was his source of pride has been taken. The light of his lamp has been extinguished. His house has been made desolate. His days have been diminished. The period of his life has approached its end; it has proved impermanent. Suffering has overcome him, the light has withdrawn and left him, and darkness has come upon him. The worm has inherited what was his. Decay has covered him. The angels who are the attendants of the Lord have cast him down. His tongue has been cut out. The light of his eyes has been destroyed. The hair of his head has been pulled out. [His] mouth has been [filled] with thirty serpents, [to] devour him. These are their [names]:[46]

The first is Distance from [God].
[The second] is Evil Envy.
The [third] is . . . .
The [fourth] is . . . .
(4b) The fifth is Jealousy.
The sixth is Cruelty.
The seventh is Vanity.
The eighth [is] Strife.
The [ninth] is Gossip.
The tenth is . . . .
The eleventh is Slander.
The twelfth is Hypocrisy.
The thirteenth is . . . .
The fourteenth is . . . .
The fifteenth is Greed.
The sixteenth is Cursing.
The seventeenth is Wrath.
The eighteenth is Treachery.
The nineteenth is Deceit.
The twentieth is the Lying Tongue.
The twenty-first is Arrogance.
The twenty-second is Scorn.
The twenty-third is Falsehood.
The twenty-fourth is Deviousness.
The twenty-fifth is Foolishness.
The twenty-sixth is Carelessness.

The twenty-seventh is Toughness Against Truth.
The twenty-eighth is Guile.
The twenty-ninth is Avarice,
The thirtieth is [Godlessness].

[These] are the thirty serpents that [were sent to] devour Judas [Iscariot. These are the] thirty [terrors] . . . . . ."[47]

(5a) These are the curses the Savior [uttered against Judas] in hell.

Judas's Life Parallels the Story of Oedipus

Golden Legend 45[48]

Matthias took the place of Judas, the traitor, among the apostles—but first let us briefly consider the birth and origin of Judas himself.

It is related in a certain—albeit apocryphal—account that there lived in Jerusalem a man named Ruben, who was also called Simon,[49] from the tribe of Judah or, according to Jerome, from the tribe of Issachar, who had a wife named Ciborea.

One night, after they had performed their marital duty, Ciborea fell asleep and had a dream. What she saw utterly terrified her. With groans and sighs she recounted the dream to her husband: "I dreamed that I gave birth to a diabolical son who became the instrument of ruin for our entire race."

"An abominable thing you say, unfit for words," Ruben replied. "You must be deluded by some bewitching spirit."

She said, "If I feel that I have become pregnant and bear a son, there is no room for doubt: that was no bewitching spirit, but a true revelation."

When, after a time, she gave birth to a son, the child's parents were stricken with fear, and began to reflect hard on what to do with him. They shuddered at the thought of killing their own son, but neither were they inclined to bring up the destroyer of their own race; so they put him in a basket and exposed him to the elements on the sea.

The surging sea drove him to an island called Scarioth. From this island Judas was called "Iscariot." Now, the queen of that place, who was without children herself, went to the seashore for a walk. When she saw the basket being cast about in the waves, she directed that it be opened. Finding a boy of lovely appearance inside, she heaved a sigh and said, "Oh, if only I were cheered by the consolation of such offspring, that I might not be robbed of a successor to my reign!"

So she had the boy brought up in secret and feigned her own pregnancy, and at last she pretended that she had given birth to a son. Throughout the entire kingdom this report circulated and was greeted with great fanfare. Sovereigns rejoiced exceedingly on behalf of her recognized offspring, and the people reveled in unspeakable joy.

She had him brought up in accordance with royal magnificence. But shortly thereafter the queen conceived by her husband and, coming to term, gave birth to a son. When the boys had grown up a little, they often played with each other, but time and again Judas would aggravate and injure the royal child and bring him to tears. The queen, distressed at the situation, and knowing that Judas was no relation of hers, beat him repeatedly, but even so he did not put an end to his ill treatment of the boy.

At last the whole matter was laid bare, and it was revealed that Judas was not the true son of the queen, but had been discovered by her. Upon learning of this, Judas burned with shame, and in secret he came upon his own supposed brother, the son of the king, and killed him. Fearing the penalty of his capital crime, he ran away with his subordinates to Jerusalem and delivered himself up to the court of Pilate, then procurator; and since birds of a feather really do flock together, Pilate found Judas to be eminently agreeable to his own character and so developed a powerful affection for him. He put Judas in charge of his entire court, and everything was dealt out according to his pleasure.

One day Pilate was looking out from his palace onto a certain orchard, and he was seized by so great a desire for its fruit that he could scarcely withdraw his gaze. The orchard belonged to Ruben, the father of Judas, but neither Judas knew his father nor Ruben his son. Ruben thought his son had perished in the surging sea, and Judas was wholly ignorant of the identity of his father and his fatherland. Thereupon Pilate summoned Judas and said, "So fierce a desire for that fruit has taken possession of me that, if I am kept from it, I will breathe my last!"

Roused to action, Judas leapt into the orchard and hastily began picking apples. Just then Ruben arrived and discovered Judas picking his apples. The two entered into a violent dispute and heaped on abuse, and from abuse they came to blows and afflicted injuries upon each other. At last Judas struck Ruben with a rock flush on that part of the head where the nape joins the neck, and killed him. Then he brought the fruit to Pilate and recounted the entire incident.

As the day waned and night came on, Ruben was found dead, believed to have been overtaken by a sudden demise. Thereupon Pilate handed over to Judas all of Ruben's property and joined him in wedlock with Ruben's wife, Ciborea. One day, however, Ciborea was sighing heavily, and Judas, her husband, made repeated inquiries as to what was the matter.

"Alas, I am the most wretched of all women!" she replied. "I plunged my newborn child into the surging sea and found my husband snatched up by death. But Pilate—my heart breaks even to say it—has heaped pains upon pains: he has given me in marriage, miserable though I am, and joined me in wedlock, however unwilling, to you."

She proceeded to recount the whole story about that child, and Judas related all that had happened to him. So it was revealed that Judas had married his mother and killed his father. Overcome by remorse, on Ciborea's advice he approached our Lord Jesus Christ and begged mercy for his transgressions.[50]

So much for the foregoing apocryphal account. Should it be repeated? I leave it to the reader to decide, although really it should be rejected rather than defended.

The Lord, in any case, made Judas his disciple and chose him as one of the apostles. So cherished and beloved of the Lord did Judas become that he made him his treasurer—a treasurer, however, whom he would soon endure as a traitor. Judas, you see, was responsible for the cash box, and he would constantly pilfer the donations given to Christ. At the time of the passion of the Lord, he became greatly aggrieved that a perfume worth three hundred denarii had not been sold—he would have pocketed the money, naturally—and he left and sold the Lord for thirty denarii. Each one was worth ten ordinary denarii, and in this way he made up for the loss of the three hundred denarii from the perfume. On another interpretation, Judas was in the habit of pilfering a tenth of the contributions made to Christ, and so he sold the Lord for a tenth of what he would have made from selling the perfume, namely, thirty denarii.[51]

Overcome with remorse, he returned the money and went and hanged himself with a noose.[52] His midsection burst open as he was hanging there, and his entrails spilled out everywhere.[53] But he was spared from vomiting through his mouth: it would have been wrong for his mouth to be so horribly befouled, since it had touched so glorious a face as Christ's. It was proper, though, that his entrails had burst out and fallen—they had conceived the betrayal, after all—and that his throat, from which had issued the voice of betrayal, had been tightened by the noose. It was in mid-air, moreover, that Judas died, so that the man who had been an affront to angels in heaven and people on earth might be separated from the heavenly and human spheres and mingle with the demons in midair.

After the ascension and before Pentecost, when the apostles were together in the upper room, Peter saw that the number of the twelve apostles had been diminished by one; and the Lord had chosen the apostles precisely in this number, to preach faith in the trinity in the four regions of the earth. He arose in the midst of the brethren and said, "Brothers, we should find a replacement for Judas, someone to bear witness with us to the resurrection of Christ. As Christ said to us, 'You shall be my witnesses in Jerusalem and in all of Judea and Samaria and even to the end of the earth.' And since an eyewitness alone should bring forth testimony, one of these men ought to be chosen—one of these who were with us constantly and witnessed the miracles of the Lord and heard his teaching."

They nominated two of the seventy-two disciples: Joseph, surnamed "the Just" because of his holiness, and Matthias, whose merits are left silent in the record—sufficient commendation for him is the fact that he was chosen as one of the apostles. Lifting their hands in prayer they said, "Lord, you know the hearts of us all. Reveal which one of these two you have chosen, to take the place of this ministry and apostleship left vacant by Judas."

The lots were cast. The lot fell on Matthias, and he was added to the eleven apostles.[54]

CHAPTER SEVEN

Traitors Before Judas

THE FIGURE OF THE FRIEND WHO TURNS A FRIEND IN AND betrays him is familiar from literature other than the Judas texts. Three such literary figures or sets of figures are well known and especially appropriate for the current discussion: Judah and the other brothers of Joseph in *Genesis* 37, the fickle friend of the psalmist in *Psalm* 41, and Melanthius the goatherd in Homer's *Odyssey*. Texts that describe these traitors are presented in this chapter.

In these three accounts—two in Hebrew literature and one in a Greek epic—friends or family members are unfaithful and act as traitors, and their stories, which resonate well with the story of Judas, raise the question of whether the story of Judas Iscariot, in part or as a whole, could be a piece of religious fiction derived from a previous story of betrayal. In *Genesis* 37, Joseph is sold to merchants on their way to Egypt by his own brothers, the forebears of the twelve tribes of Israel, and the brother who comes up with the idea of selling Joseph is Judah—named Judas in the Greek of the Septuagint. The price for Joseph is twenty pieces of silver, ten short of the price set for Jesus. Later in the story, in *Genesis 44*, it is Judah who, in remorse, offers to surrender himself to Joseph, now established as a powerful figure in Egypt. John Shelby Spong, in *Liberating the Gospels,* sees a close connection between the two stories of betrayal, and he suggests that elements from the story of the betrayal of Joseph, along with other hints in the Jewish Scriptures, were brought together in the New Testament tradition to create a midrash—a narrative compiled from sacred scripture—on Jesus being handed over.

In *Psalm 41,* the psalmist complains that he has been treated badly by a villainous friend, who shared his food but lifted up his heel against him (v. 9). *John 13:18* cites *Psalm 41:9* directly in order to indicate that scripture is being fulfilled in the events surrounding Jesus and Judas. In Homer's *Odyssey,* Odysseus must deal with the treachery of Melanthius the goatherd. Melanthius conspires against Odysseus with the suitors who have come together in Ithaca, and he gathers arms from the storeroom (twelve shields, helmets, and spears) to distribute to the suitors. For his treachery Melanthius is captured and hanged. He is strung up from the rafters, and after Odysseus finishes dealing with the suitors, he and his comrades punish Melanthius by cutting off parts of his body, including his genitals, which they toss to the dogs. So, Melanthius comes to a bloody and gruesome end.

In his book *The Homeric Epics and the Gospel of Mark,* Dennis MacDonald refers to the story of Melanthius and focuses upon a number of the details—acting with duplicity, gathering sets of arms, being hanged, and dying in a ghastly fashion—in support of his theory that Mark (and other Christian authors after Mark) fashioned the figure of Judas on the basis of Melanthius in the *Odyssey*. According to MacDonald, Judas Iscariot is not a historical character but a literary one, a reconfigured Melanthius. We might be inclined to draw similar conclusions with regard to the creative contributions of the stories of betrayal in Hebrew literature.

However we evaluate the precise relationship of the Judas texts to these other stories of betrayal, Judah and his brothers, the false friend of the psalmist, and Melanthius the goatherd may assume places of distinction alongside Judas Iscariot. With Judas, these all are memorable characters who are portrayed, fairly or not, as among the most engaging traitors we may encounter in ancient literature.

Judah and the Other Brothers of Joseph

Genesis 37:2–36 [1]

(2) Joseph, a young man seventeen years old, was tending the flock with his brothers, the sons of Bilhah and Zilpah, the wives of his father (Israel, or Jacob), and he brought back a negative report about them to their father. (3) Israel loved Joseph more than any other of his sons, because he was the son of his old age, and he made a fancy robe for him. (4) When his brothers noticed that their father loved him more than any of them, they hated him, and they had nothing good to say to him.

(5) Now, Joseph had a dream, and when he told it to his brothers, they hated him all the more. (6) He said to them, "Let me tell you about the dream I had. (7) Look, we were binding sheaves

of grain in the field when my sheaf rose and stood up, and your sheaves gathered around my sheaf and bowed down to it."

(8) His brothers said to him, "Are you really going to rule over us? Or will you dominate us?" And they hated him even more because of his dreams and his words.

(9) Then he had another dream, and he told it to his brothers. He said, "Look, I had another dream, and the sun, the moon, and eleven stars were bowing down to me."

(10) When he told his father as well as his brothers, his father scolded him and said to him, "What is this dream you had? Will your mother and I and your brothers really come and bow down to the ground before you?" (11) His brothers were jealous of him, but his father kept the incident in mind.

(12) Well, his brothers went to pasture their father's flock near Shechem. (13) Israel said to Joseph, "Aren't your brothers pasturing the flock at Shechem? Come, I am going to send you to them."

"Fine with me," he answered.

(14) So he said to him, "Go and see if everything is all right with your brothers and the flock, and send word back to me." And he sent him from the Valley of Hebron, and he came to Shechem. (15) A man found him wandering through the fields, and he asked him, "What are you looking for?"

(16) He said, "I am looking for my brothers. Could you tell me where they are pasturing the flock?"

(17) The man replied, "They have left this area, for I heard them say, 'Let's go to Dothan.'"

So Joseph followed his brothers and found them at Dothan. (18) They saw him a long ways away, and before he reached them, they plotted against him in order to kill him.

(19) They said to each other, "Here comes that dreamer. (20) Come, let's kill him and throw him into one of the cisterns, and say that a wild animal devoured him. Then we'll see what becomes of his dreams."

(21) When Reuben heard this, he tried to deliver him from their hands. He said to them, "Let's not take his life. (22) Shed no blood." Reuben said, "Throw him into this cistern out here in the wilderness, but don't lay a hand on him." He said this so that he might rescue him from their hands and bring him back to his father.

(23) As a result, when Joseph came to his brothers, they stripped his robe from him—the fancy robe he was wearing—and they took him and threw him into the cistern. The cistern was empty, with no water in it.

(25) As they sat down to eat, they looked up and saw a caravan of Ishmaelites on their way from Gilead. Their camels were loaded down with spices, balm, and myrrh, and they were taking them down to Egypt.

(26) Judah[2] said to his brothers, "What good will it do us if we kill our brother and conceal his blood? (27) Come, let's sell him to the Ishmaelites, and not lay our hands on him, for he's our brother, our own flesh and blood." His brothers were in agreement.

(28) So, when the Midianite merchants came by, they[3] hauled Joseph up out of the cistern, and they sold him to the Ishmaelites for twenty shekels of silver.[4] The Ishmaelites took Joseph to Egypt.

(29) Reuben returned to the cistern and saw that Joseph was not there, and he tore his clothes. (30) He went back to his brothers and said, "The lad is gone. Where can I go now?"

(31) Then they took Joseph's robe, slaughtered a goat, and dipped the robe in the blood. (32) They took the fancy robe back

to their father and said, "We found this. Take a look at it and see whether or not it is your son's robe."

(33) He recognized it and said, "It is my son's robe. A wild animal has devoured him, and Joseph must have been torn to pieces."

(34) Then Jacob tore his clothes and put on sackcloth, and he mourned for his son for many days. (35) All his sons and all his daughters rose up to comfort him, but he would not be comforted. He said, "No, I'll go to my grave[5] mourning for my son." And thus his father wept for him.

(36) In the meantime, the Midianites sold Joseph in Egypt to Potiphar, an official of the pharaoh, the captain of the guard.

The Friend of the Psalmist

Psalm 41[6]

(1) *Fortunate is one who has regard for the weak;*
on the day of trouble Yahweh delivers him.
(2) *Yahweh protects him and sustains his life;*
he blesses him in the land;
you do not abandon him to the will of his foes.
(3) *Yahweh sustains him on his sickbed;*
you restore him from his bed of illness.
(4) *As for me, I said, "Yahweh, have mercy on me;*
heal me, for I have sinned against you."
(5) *My foes say of me, with malice,*
"When will he die and his name be lost?"
(6) *And when someone comes to see me,*
he speaks worthless words, his heart embracing slander;

then he leaves and spreads it around.
(7) All who hate me whisper together against me;
they imagine the worst about me.
(8) They say, "A horrible malady has come upon him;
he will never again arise from where he lies."
(9) Even my close friend, whom I trusted,
who ate of my bread, has lifted up his heel against me.[7]
(10) But you, Yahweh, have mercy on me,
and raise me up, that I may pay them back.
(11) By this I know you are pleased with me,
that my foe has not overcome me.
(12) No, you have upheld me in my integrity,
and placed me in your presence forever.
(13) Blessed be Yahweh, God of Israel,
from everlasting to everlasting.
Amen and Amen.

Melanthius the Goatherd

Homer, Odyssey 22.126–202, 473–76[8]

A back door stood in the well-wrought wall,
and by the threshold's edge in the well-built hall
led a path to the alley, held by well-fitted doors;
and the good swineherd,[9] *at Odysseus's orders, stood*
nearby to guard the path, the one and only approach.
Agelaos addressed them all, proposing a plan:
"Comrades! Couldn't someone sneak out the back
door and tell the people, and sound the cry at once?

Then, right soon, this man would shoot his last arrows."
The goatherd, Melanthius, spoke to him in turn:
"Impossible, Zeus-bred Agelaos! For dreadfully close
stand the court's fine doors, and the mouth of the alley is
hard to force. A single man, if he be strong, could hold back
us all. No, come now, let me bring you arms to put on
from the chamber: inside, I think, and nowhere else the two
have stowed the weapons, Odysseus and his resplendent son." [10]
Speaking so, Melanthius, herder of goats, crept into
Odysseus's chamber through the clefts in the hall,
and from there took out twelve shields, twelve spears,
twelve bronze-tipped helms with thick horsehair crests;
and he left with them, and gave them at once to the
suitors. Odysseus's knees and heart trembled when he
saw them donning arms and brandishing long spears
in their hands, so great did the task appear to him. [11]
Forthwith he sped winged words to Telemachus:
"Telemachus, one of the women in the halls must be
rousing cheerless battle against us two—or
Melanthius." Astute Telemachus replied to him,
"I, father, I myself erred in this—no one else is to
blame—I, who left the chamber's door, fitted
closely, ajar. The suitors' look-out was better.
Now go, noble Eumaeus, shut the door of the chamber,
and see if it's one of the women who is doing this,
or Dolius's son, Melanthius. I bet he's the one."
With such words were they speaking to each other
when the goatherd, Melanthius, returned to the chamber
to get fine arms. But the good swineherd noticed,

and at once addressed Odysseus who was standing near:
"Zeus-sprung son of Laertes, resourceful Odysseus,
that bane of our existence, just whom we thought, is going
back to the storeroom. Tell me—no hedging!—should I
kill him, if I gain the upper hand, or bring him
here to you, to pay recompense for the many
offenses he has contrived in your house?"
To him Odysseus of many wiles said in reply:
"Telemachus and I will keep the illustrious suitors at bay
within the halls, fume all they might; but you two,
hogtie him by his feet and his hands, and cast him
into the chamber. Bind planks behind his back,
and once you have fastened a twisted rope to him,
hoist him up to a high column, all the way to the rafters—
so the longer he lives, the worse the pains."
So he spoke. They heard him well and obeyed,
and went to the chamber, escaping his notice inside;
and while he hunted for weapons in the room's recesses,
the two stood and waited, flanking the doorposts.
When Melanthius, herder of goats, crossed the threshold,
a lovely helmet in one hand, and a broad old shield
in the other, caked with mold—it was the hero's, Laertes',
which he bore in his youth, but by that time had been put
away, and the stitches of its straps had unraveled—
they sprang upon him and seized him. Dragging him in by
his hair, they threw him to the ground, on the floor, despairing
in soul, and bound together feet and hands with a heartrending
bond, hogtying him well—no escape—as ordered by
Laertes' son, long-suffering shining Odysseus;

and they fastened a twisted rope to him and hoisted
him up to a high column, all the way to the rafters.[12]
You prodded him, swineherd Eumaeus, with stinging
taunts: "Now, all the night through you will keep
watch, Melanthius, lying in a soft bed, as becomes you;
nor will you miss early-born dawn, rising from Ocean's
streams on her golden throne—the time you're wont to bring
goats to the suitors, to be busied about the feast in the halls."
There he was left, racked in a baneful bond;
and the two, donning their armor, shut the shining door and
rejoined clever Odysseus with his intricate schemes.

They led out Melanthius through the gate and the courtyard.
They lopped off his nose and his ears with pitiless
bronze, sliced off his balls—to throw raw to the dogs—and
chopped off his hands and his feet, fuming with fury.[13]

NOTES

Introduction: The Vilification and Redemption of a Disciple of Jesus

1. For some of the more recent studies of and texts about Judas Iscariot, see Bart D. Ehrman, *The Lost Gospel of Judas Iscariot*; Rodolphe Kasser, Marvin Meyer, Gregor Wurst, and François Gaudard, eds., *Codex Tchacos*; Rodolphe Kasser, Marvin Meyer, and Gregor Wurst, eds., *The Gospel of Judas*; William Klassen, *Judas: Betrayer or Friend of Jesus?*; Hans-Josef Klauck, *Judas—Ein Jünger des Herrn*; Herbert Krosney, *The Lost Gospel*; Hyam Maccoby, *Judas Iscariot and the Myth of Jewish Evil*; Kim Paffenroth, *Judas: Images of the Lost Disciple*; Elaine H. Pagels and Karen L. King, *Reading Judas*; James M. Robinson, *The Secrets of Judas*; and N. T. Wright, *Judas and the Gospel of Jesus*.

2. See Chapter 1.

3. Cf. Simon Iscariot as the father of Judas according to *John* 6:71; 13:2, 26.

4. See Chapter 6.

5. Krosney, *The Lost Gospel*, 10.

6. See Krosney, *The Lost Gospel*.

7. For an account of the process of restoration and conservation, see the essay by Rodolphe Kasser in Kasser, Meyer, Wurst, and Gaudard, eds., *Codex Tchacos*, 1–25; and in Kasser, Meyer, and Wurst, eds., *The Gospel of Judas*, 47–76.

8. See Kasser, Meyer, and Wurst, eds., *The Gospel of Judas*, 183–85.

9. For a codicological analysis of Codex Tchacos, see the essay by Gregor Wurst in Kasser, Meyer, Wurst, and Gaudard, eds., *Codex Tchacos*, 27–33.

10. See Chapter 2. Other Gnostic texts that refer to Judas are presented in Chapters 3–5.

11. On the current discussion of the terms and themes of Gnostic thought, see Karen L. King, *What Is Gnosticism?*; Bentley Layton, "Prolegomena to the Study of Ancient Gnosticism"; Antti Marjanen, ed., *Was There a Gnostic Religion?*; Marvin

Notes

Meyer, *The Gnostic Discoveries;* Birger A. Pearson, *Gnosticism and Christianity in Roman and Coptic Egypt;* and Michael A. Williams, *Rethinking "Gnosticism."*

12. *Gospel of Judas* 33.
13. *Gospel of Judas* 35.
14. *Gospel of Judas* 47.
15. *Gospel of Judas* 56.
16. See the notes to *Gospel of Judas* 57.
17. The *Gospel of Judas* is explicitly mentioned by Irenaeus of Lyon in his work *Against Heresies* (1.31.1), which was composed around 180 CE. For the *Gospel of Judas* to be known by Irenaeus, it must have been composed some time before Irenaeus wrote his text—hence the suggestion of a date of composition for the original *Gospel of Judas* around the middle of the second century.
18. See Eusebius of Caesarea *Church History.*
19. On criticism of sacrifice in the *Gospel of Judas,* see Pagels and King, *Reading Judas.*
20. In general, on the rhetoric and politics of heresiological discussions, see King, *What Is Gnosticism?*
21. On Judas as the friend of Jesus in the *Gospel of Judas,* see Chapter 2.
22. See also William Klassen, "Judas Iscariot."
23. Klassen, *Judas: Betrayer or Friend of Jesus?* 68–69.
24. Klassen, *Judas: Betrayer or Friend of Jesus?* 74.
25. See Chapter 3.
26. *Dialogue of the Savior* 127.
27. *Dialogue of the Savior* 129.
28. *Dialogue of the Savior* 131.
29. The meaning of "Iscariot" (*Iskariôth* or *Iskariôtês* in the Greek of the New Testament) has been discussed extensively by scholars, and a number of etymological theories have been proposed. Since the Hebrew *iš* means "man" (or "man of"), the word "Iscariot" has frequently been understood as a nickname indicating where Judas came from. According to this interpretation, Judas was a man of Kerioth, which may be a village in southern Judea (cf. *Joshua* 15:25, and possibly the site of Tell Qirrioth in the Negev), or Askaroth or Askar (in the vicinity of Shechem), or even just "the city," perhaps the city of Jerusalem. In support of this theory may be the similar designation of the father of Judas as Simon Iscariot in the *Gospel of John.* In addition, several times in *John* (6:71; 12:4; 13:2, 26; 14:22) there are manuscript witnesses—once, in *John* 6:71, the textual witness is the original hand of Codex Sinaiticus—that offer, as an alternative to "Iscariot," the reading *apo Karuôtou,* "from Karioth" (or the like). "Iscariot" has also been interpreted to

derive from the name of the Sicarii, the dagger-men among the Jewish partisans who engaged in acts of assassination, and thus Judas has been understood to be a member of a radical group comparable to the Zealots. Others have suggested that "Iscariot" is a form of the Hebrew *šakar* and means "false one," in reference to the betrayal of Jesus, or that "Iscariot" means "deliverer" (in the sense of one who hands someone over—cf. the Greek *paradidonai*), or that the term refers to his profession (that he grew fruit trees or was involved in dyeing with red dye). Cf. Klassen, "Judas Iscariot." Recently, in a panel discussion in Claremont, California (and through personal communication), Dennis MacDonald proposed that the term "Iscariot" may in fact come from the Greek preposition "into" (*eis*) plus the Aramaic word for city (see above), so that Judas Iscariot could mean "Judas into the City." MacDonald writes: "It is in Jerusalem that Judas betrays Jesus, and his Homeric counterpart is Melanthius, whose job it was to drive goats 'into the city' for the suitors. He also supplied them with weapons, and nearly exposed Odysseus to the suitors."

30. See Chapter 7. In general, see the discussion in John Shelby Spong, *Liberating the Gospels*, 257–76.

31. See Dennis R. MacDonald, *The Homeric Epics and the Gospel of Mark*; also *Mimesis and Intertextuality in Antiquity and Christianity*.

32. See Chapter 7.

33. Nikos Kazantzakis, *The Last Temptation of Christ*, 385–86.

Chapter One: Judas in the New Testament

1. William Klassen, *Judas: Betrayer or Friend of Jesus?* 202–3.

2. Greek *paredōka* (from *paradidonai*).

3. Greek *paredideto* (from *paradidonai*).

4. The reference is to the last supper. The translations in this chapter are based on the Greek text of the New Testament.

5. Greek *paradontos* (from *paradidonai*).

6. Greek *paredōken* (from *paradidonai*).

7. Greek *paredōka* (from *paradidonai*).

8. Perhaps "of first importance."

9. Peter.

10. Paul's proclamation that Christ appeared to the Twelve may be in conflict with New Testament gospel accounts that seem to separate Judas from the Twelve after he hands Jesus over.

11. Or "into the hills."

12. The Twelve, here and below, are a reflection of the twelve tribes of Israel.

13. This nickname is derived from Aramaic.

14. Or "Thaddaeus," here and below. *Mark* and *Matthew* list Thaddeus (some texts read Lebbaeus), and *Luke* and *Acts* list Judas the son of James. *John* 14:22 refers to Judas but not Iscariot. *John* also mentions Nathanael (1:43–51; 21:2).

15. Or "Zealot."

16. On Thaddeus and the other disciples, see the note to *Mark* 3:18.

17. Or "Zealot."

18. The *Gospel of the Ebionites* refers to the Twelve as apostles for a testimony to Israel, and it lists eight names, including Judas Iscariot, along with James and John, Simon (Peter), Andrew, Thaddeus, Simon the Zealot, "and you, Matthew."

19. On Judas the son of James and the other disciples, see the note to *Mark* 3:18. Birger Pearson reports, in "Judas Iscariot and the *Gospel of Judas*," 2, "In a forthcoming commentary on the Gospel of Mark Dennis R. MacDonald argues that Mark based his list of the twelve on an earlier list found in the sayings source Q (cf. Luke 6:12–16), to which he added the name Iscariot and the phrase 'who betrayed him.'"

20. Cf. also *Acts* 1:13, below (a list of the eleven disciples, without Judas Iscariot).

21. Greek *prodotês*.

22. Or "Lord," "Rabbi," here and below.

23. Greek *litra*, a Roman pound.

24. A denarius was the average daily wage for a laborer. Thus, three hundred denarii is about a year's wages.

25. In the same context *Matthew* 26:8 reads "The disciples."

26. See the note to *John* 12:5.

27. Cf. the parallel passage in *Matthew* 26:6–13. This story is very similar to the account of Judas's objections in the *Gospel of John*.

28. Here the text reads, "Amen I tell you."

29. On being paid in silver, cf. the silver coins of *Matthew* 26:15, and the note.

30. On thirty silver coins, or thirty pieces of silver, cf. *Zechariah* 11:12–13 (cited at *Matthew* 27:9), where thirty pieces of silver are to be paid for a shepherd king and thrown to a potter. In *Exodus* 21:32 thirty pieces (or shekels) of silver are said to be the price to be paid if a slave is gored by an ox.

31. See the note to *Matthew* 26:15.

32. The New Testament story of the washing of the disciples' feet is told only in the *Gospel of John*.

33. "Amen, amen."

34. *Psalm* 41:9. See Chapter 7.
35. "Amen, amen."
36. "Amen."
37. Cf. *Psalm* 41:9.
38. Or "Son of Man," here and below.
39. As here in the *Gospel of Mark*, the New Testament gospels—and theologians since the days of the early church—struggle with the tension between the crucifixion as a part of the divine plan and the crucifixion as a moment of human tragedy brought about by the one who handed Jesus over.
40. "Amen."
41. Cf. *Psalm* 41:9.
42. Cf. *Psalm* 41:9.
43. "Amen, amen."
44. The disciple Jesus loved, or the beloved disciple, is commonly assumed to be John the son of Zebedee in the *Gospel of John*. In the *Gospel of John* and other gospels, including gospels outside the New Testament, other disciples are also considered to be beloved, including Lazarus, Mary Magdalene, Judas Thomas, James the Just—and perhaps Judas Iscariot in the *Gospel of Judas.*
45. Cf. *Psalm* 41:9.
46. The prayer of Jesus in chap. 17, sometimes called the high-priestly prayer, is found only in the *Gospel of John* in the New Testament.
47. Or "son bound for destruction." Cf., e.g., 2 *Thessalonians* 2:3; *Proverbs* 24:22.
48. On the account of Judas handing Jesus over to the authorities, cf. the story of Melanthius in Homer's *Odyssey* (below, Chapter 7).
49. On Judas kissing Jesus, cf. Joab, King David's military commander, taking Amasa by the beard, preparing to kiss him, and plunging a dagger into his belly (2 *Samuel* 20:10). In general, on Judas handing Jesus over for money, cf. the account of Joseph being handed over by his brothers, and particularly Judah—Judas—in *Genesis* 37. John Shelby Spong describes the similarities in the two stories and suggests a midrashic connection: "In the Jewish tradition, there was one other major story in which a gigantic Jewish hero was betrayed or handed over to the enemy. That was the story in the *Book of Genesis* (37–50). In that story the 'handing over' was done by a group of twelve who later became known as the leaders of the twelve tribes of Israel. In the Jesus story, the 'handing over' also came out of a group of twelve who were designated the leaders of the Church that came to call itself the new Israel. In both stories the handing over or betrayal was into the hands of gentiles, and death was the presumed result of each act of treachery. In both stories God intervened to reverse that presumed outcome. In both stories

the hero was imprisoned for a time—Joseph in the pharaoh's jail, Jesus in Joseph's tomb. In both stories money was given to the traitors—twenty pieces of silver for Joseph, thirty pieces of silver for Jesus. Not lost in this analysis was the fact that one of the twelve brothers of Joseph who urged the others to seek money for their act of betrayal was named Judah or Judas (*Genesis* 37:26–27). In the light of these similarities, it is hard not to doubt that there was some intermingling of the stories" (*Liberating the Gospels*, 267). On the *Genesis* story of betrayal, see below, Chapter 7.

50. Or "My friend, do what you have come for."

51. On Judas kissing Jesus in this scene, see the note to *Mark* 14:46.

52. On Judas kissing Jesus, see the note to *Mark* 14:46.

53. Or "Jesus of Nazareth," here and below.

54. Cf. *John* 6:39; 10:28; 17:12. In the account of Jesus being handed over to the authorities in the *Gospel of John*, Jesus remains in complete control of the situation.

55. On thirty silver coins, see the note to *Matthew* 26:15.

56. Lit., "You see to it."

57. Cf. *Zechariah* 11:13: thirty pieces of silver are thrown into the house of the Lord.

58. Cf. *2 Samuel* 17:23: Ahithophel, an advisor to David who joins the rebellion against the king, hangs himself. On Judas being hanged, perhaps cf. the account of the crucifixion of Judas in the *Gospel of Barnabas* (below, Chapter 6). The account of the death of Judas in *Acts* 1:18 is quite different from *Matthew*'s story, in spite of attempts to harmonize them (cf. *Golden Legend* 45, below, Chapter 6).

59. Cf. *Acts* 1:19, where the field is called Akeldama. Tradition associates this site with the area of the Valley of Hinnom (in Greek, Gehenna), south of Jerusalem, where the worship of Molech took place. In *Jeremiah* 19:1–13, Jeremiah describes this area as near the Potsherd Gate of Jerusalem (sometimes said to be the same as the Dung Gate), where potters were active. During the first century CE this area was used as a dump, and it was associated with judgment and punishment in hell. Cf. the popular use of the term "Gehenna" to the present day.

60. *Zechariah* 11:12–13; cf. *Jeremiah* 18:1–4 (on seeing a potter); 19:1–13 (on buying a jar and going to the area of the Potsherd Gate); 32:6–9 (on buying a field with silver coins).

61. In Jerusalem.

62. A list of the eleven disciples (without Judas Iscariot). See the lists of the Twelve above.

63. Lit., "Men, brothers," here and below.

64. Or "field," "small farm."

65. In the Jewish Scriptures and elsewhere, bad people are frequently depicted dying badly; such is the case, for example, in accounts of the deaths of Eglon, Sisera, and Korah, Dathan, and Abiram, among others. According to 2 *Samuel* 20:10, Amasa, active at the time of the conspiracy against King David, was stabbed to death by Joab, and his intestines spilled out on the ground. In the Jewish tractate *Hullin* (56b), it is said, "A gentile saw how a man fell from the roof to the ground, so that his belly burst and his bowels came out" (cited in Ernst Haenchen, *The Acts of the Apostles*, 160). In Greek literature (Apian *Civil Wars*), Cato the Younger committed suicide at the time of the Roman civil war by stabbing himself with his sword and then, later, ripping out his intestines. In Homer, Dennis MacDonald observes, falling forward, face first, in death, can be a sign of the cowardice of someone who is running away and is attacked from behind. The account of the death of Judas by hanging in *Matthew* 27:5 is a different story altogether from what is given in *Acts*, though some have tried—and still try—to harmonize the two accounts. Cf. the *Golden Legend*, below, Chapter 6.

66. Cf. *Matthew* 27:7–8. The name Akeldama comes from Aramaic. See the note to *Matthew* 27:7–8.

67. *Psalm* 69:25 (68:26, Septuagint).

68. *Psalm* 109:8 (108:8, Septuagint). The Greek word used here for "position as overseer" (or "office of bishop") is *episkopê*.

Chapter Two: The Gospel of Judas

1. Codex Tchacos 3: 33,1–58,29. This translation is based on the Coptic text in Rodolphe Kasser, Marvin Meyer, Gregor Wurst, and François Gaudard, eds., *Codex Tchacos*. Cf. also Bart D. Ehrman, *The Lost Gospel of Judas Iscariot*; Rodolphe Kasser, Marvin Meyer, and Gregor Wurst, eds., *The Gospel of Judas*; and Elaine H. Pagels and Karen L. King, *Reading Judas*.

2. Lit., "eight days." Cf. also the octave, an eight-day festival in the liturgical year.

3. Or "before he observed Passover."

4. On Jesus calling his disciples, cf. *Matthew* 10:1–4; *Mark* 3:13–19; *Luke* 6:12–16.

5. On Jesus seen as a child, cf. *Secret Book of John* II, 2; *Revelation of Paul* 18; *Gospel of Thomas* 4; *Acts of John* 88; Hippolytus *Refutation of All Heresies* 6.42.2. The word "child" could also be translated "apparition" or even "veil."

6. Or "offering a prayer of thanksgiving," perhaps even "celebrating the eucharist" (Coptic *eu'reukharisti*).

7. On the laughter of Jesus, see, besides the *Gospel of Judas,* the *Secret Book of John; Wisdom of Jesus Christ* III, 91–92; *Second Discourse of Great Seth* 56; *Revelation of Peter* 81; Basilides, in Irenaeus of Lyon *Against Heresies* 1.24.4; perhaps "Round Dance of the Cross" 96.

8. Or "eucharist."

9. The disciples profess that Jesus is the son of their own God, who is the creator of this world, but they are mistaken.

10. Or "Amen (*hamên*) I say to you," here and below.

11. The restoration is tentative; also possible is "[his servants]."

12. Lit., "along with your souls."

13. Cf. *Gospel of Thomas* 46.

14. Aeon, here and below.

15. Barbelo is the divine Mother and the first emanation of the divine in a number of Sethian texts, e.g., the *Secret Book of John.* The name Barbelo may derive from Hebrew and may mean is "God in four"—i.e., God as known through the tetragrammaton, the ineffable name of God, YHWH.

16. Cf. *Gospel of Thomas* 13:4.

17. Lit., "he."

18. Or "but that you will go."

19. Here the text seems to indicate that Judas is not destined to go at once to the realm above but that he must stay here below to accomplish what needs to be done—even though it will cause him to grieve. Cf. also *Gospel of Judas* 46.

20. This seems to be a reference to the appointment of Matthias to replace Judas in the circle of the disciples according to *Acts* 1:15–26.

21. The restoration is tentative. Perhaps read "when."

22. Or "Master" (Coptic *pjois*).

23. Aeons.

24. "Amen."

25. Aeon.

26. The stars are discussed at length later in the *Gospel of Judas.*

27. Lit., "great [dreams]."

28. This fragmentary section may conceivably be restored to refer to premonitions the disciples experience of the arrest of Jesus in the garden of Gethsemane and what happens thereafter, when the disciples run for their lives.

29. Or "building." The reference is to the Jewish temple in Jerusalem.

30. Probably thought to be the name of either God or Jesus.

31. The text inadvertently repeats the phrase "at the altar" (dittography).

32. Or "fast." The restoration is tentative; but see *Gospel of Judas* 40.

33. Or "their deficient actions," "their faulty actions," "their wrong actions"—the Coptic reads *šôôt*, which functions as a technical term for the deficiency of light in many Gnostic texts. The word *šôôt* may also be translated "sacrifice."

34. If "deficiency" is the preferred translation of *šôôt*, there may be a contrast here between fullness and deficiency.

35. "Amen."

36. On trees and fruit, cf. also *Gospel of Judas* 43; *Revelation of Adam* 76; 85.

37. The restoration is tentative; also possible is "[The . . . overseer (or bishop)]" or "[The . . . minister (or deacon)]."

38. Or "[those who fornicate]."

39. Or "fast." Cf. *Gospel of Judas* 38.

40. Or "a priest."

41. Or "Lord of the universe."

42. Possibly restore to read "[ensnared]," "[quarreling]," "[in a struggle]," "[deficient]," "[diminished]," or the like.

43. About fifteen lines missing.

44. This teaching about people and the stars assigned to them seems to derive from Plato; cf. *Timaeus* 41d–42b. On Judas's star, cf. *Gospel of Judas* 57.

45. About seventeen lines missing.

46. Aeon.

47. Lit., "he" or "it." The antecedent of the pronoun is unclear.

48. Or perhaps "to drink of."

49. Or "[generation]."

50. Coptic *[hrabb]ei*, which is restored with some confidence because of the other instances of the word "rabbi" in Codex Tchacos. In the *Gospel of Judas*, the usual word translated "master" as a title for Jesus is Coptic *sah*.

51. The word "seed" is added in the translation for the sake of clarification.

52. Here the pronoun translated "its" is plural. On this saying, cf. the parable of the sower in *Matthew* 13:1–23; *Mark* 4:1–20; *Luke* 8:4–15; *Gospel of Thomas* 9.

53. Or "generation."

54. Sophia. Here Wisdom or Sophia may refer to the personified figure of Wisdom or serve as a more general reference to wisdom—"corruptible wisdom."

55. Aeons.

56. "Amen."

57. Or "daimon," "demon." Cf. the role of the spirit or daimon of Socrates in Plato's *Symposium*. Here Judas is described as the thirteenth. According to Irenaeus

of Lyon (*Against Heresies* 1.3.3), some Valentinians counted Judas as the twelfth apostle, and the apostasy of the twelfth apostle then may be related among such Valentinians to the fall of Sophia, who is considered the twelfth aeon. In Sethian tradition it sometimes is suggested that the number thirteen may have a particular significance when attached to aeons, and in the *Holy Book of the Great Invisible Spirit* and *Zostrianos*, the thirteen aeons can be understood to describe the world below, with the ruler of the world positioned within it, presumably holding court from the thirteenth aeon. On the possible interpretation of Judas as a demon, cf. Judas as a devil in the *Gospel of John*.

58. Or, reading with Jacques van der Vliet, "Judas and the Stars," 144–45, "a single room."

59. Two lines missing. Judas is speaking the following sentence in his account.

60. Or "the holy."

61. Aeon.

62. Aeons.

63. Archons.

64. A line and a half missing.

65. Or "but that you will go."

66. Lit., "What is the advantage that I have received?"

67. Or "from." Both translations are grammatically possible. If the phrase is translated "from that generation," then "that generation" may be understood to designate a human generation. Or Judas being set apart "from that generation" could mean that Judas is assigned a role, in this world of mortality, apart from the realm of the holy generation. On Judas being set apart from the disciples, cf. *Gospel of Judas* 35.

68. Lit., "you will come to rule."

69. This remains a difficult passage, and it may be possible to understand that Jesus is telling Judas that the others will try to do something to him so that—as the text seems to say—"you may not ascend up to the holy [generation]" (cf. the use of the Coptic negative third future). Such an understanding of this passage, however, probably must assume that some letters or words have been inadvertently omitted from the Coptic text.

70. The reading is uncertain. Perhaps read "has seen"?

71. Aeon, here and below.

72. Or "a."

73. The highest expression of the divine is frequently called the Great Invisible Spirit in Sethian texts.

74. Cf. *1 Corinthians* 2:9; *Gospel of Thomas* 17; *Dialogue of the Savior* 140.

75. Or "it"—i.e., the Spirit.

76. Or "assistant," "helper," here and below.

77. Cf. the four luminaries, often named Harmozel, Oroiael, Daveithai, and Eleleth, in other Sethian texts.

78. Aeon.

79. Aeons.

80. Aeons.

81. Cf. *Eugnostos the Blessed* III, 88–89; *Wisdom of Jesus Christ* III, 113; *On the Origin of the World* 105–6.

82. Aeons.

83. Cf. *Eugnostos the Blessed* III, 83–84.

84. Aeons.

85. I.e., in the cosmos.

86. Aeon.

87. Gnosis.

88. Cf. Eleleth in other Sethian texts.

89. On the creator God with eyes flashing, cf. *Secret Book of John* II, 10.

90. On Sophia of matter defiled with blood, cf. *Holy Book of the Great Invisible Spirit* III, 56–57.

91. On Nebro or Nebruel, cf. *Holy Book of the Great Invisible Spirit* III, 57. In the *Gospel of Judas* Nebro is referred to without the honorific suffix –el. Here Nebro is said to mean "rebel," and Nebro may be related to Nimrod (Greek *Nebrôd*), the legendary character in ancient Middle Eastern traditions (cf. *Genesis* 10:8–12; *1 Chronicles* 1:10). It has been suggested that the name Nimrod may be connected to the Hebrew word for "rebel."

92. Here and elsewhere in the text the name Sakla is spelled "Saklas."

93. The names Yaldabaoth and Sakla (or Saklas) are well-known names of the demiurge in Sethian and other texts.

94. Archons.

95. One line missing.

96. Cf. *Secret Book of John* II, 10–11; *Holy Book of the Great Invisible Spirit* III, 57–58. In the list in the *Gospel of Judas*, the second angelic power is Harmathoth; in the *Secret Book of John* and the *Holy Book of the Great Invisible Spirit*, the first two are Athoth and Harmas. Further, the apparent correlation of Seth and Christ as the first angelic power is unusual in the context of other Sethian texts. Are the names Athoth and Harmas combined in the *Gospel of Judas* to make room for this surprising reference to "[Se]th, who is called Christ"—the only specifically Christian reference in this cosmological revelation? Here Jacques van der Vliet speculates, in "Judas and the

Stars," 147–51, that this Christian reference may be based on a copyist's mistake, and that the original reading, "Seth, who is called Aries (the Ram, *krios*)," was erroneously taken to be "Seth, who is called Christ (*khristos*)."

97. Cf. *Genesis* 1:26.

98. Here the name is spelled "Sakla."

99. Archon, though the restoration is tentative.

100. Here and below this phrase reads, lit., "in a number." Could the first instance of this phrase be a case of dittography?

101. The meaning of this sentence is uncertain.

102. Or "the kingless generation," "the generation with no ruler over it"—i.e., the seed or offspring of Seth.

103. One line missing.

104. About two lines missing.

105. Plural.

106. Gnosis.

107. Plural.

108. Here the text reads *alêthôs* rather than *hamên*.

109. Or "fornicate."

110. About six and a half lines missing. Cf. *Gospel of Judas* 38; 40.

111. Here the word "and" may be repeated (a case of dittography).

112. Aeon.

113. The wandering stars are usually understood to be the planets. Here the six wandering stars are probably the five known planets (Mercury, Venus, Mars, Jupiter, Saturn) and the moon.

114. *Alêthôs.*

115. About nine lines missing.

116. *Alêthôs.*

117. Three lines missing.

118. Probably the other disciples.

119. Or "who clothes me" (Coptic *etrphorei 'mmoei*). Judas may help Jesus to rid himself of the fleshly body so that the true spiritual person within may be liberated, or else he may hand over the body that Jesus himself has vacated.

120. Or "passed by," "grown dim." The meaning is uncertain.

121. Or "mind."

122. These lines recall passages from *Psalms.*

123. *Alêthôs.*

124. About two and a half lines missing.

125. About two lines missing.

126. Archon.

127. Aeons.

128. Here Professors Sasagu Arai and Gesine Schenke Robinson suggest that "he" may refer not to Judas but to Jesus. In the Coptic text, the most natural antecedent for the pronoun "he" is Judas. Nonetheless, if "he" is thought to indicate Jesus, the transfiguration that takes place in the *Gospel of Judas* would be that of Jesus, and it could be understood in the text that the spiritual person of Jesus returns through the transfiguration to the realm above and his fleshly body that is left behind in this world below is handed over to the authorities to be crucified.

129. About five lines missing. On the transfiguration of Judas (or Jesus), cf. the transfiguration of Jesus in the New Testament gospels and *Book of Allogenes* 61–62ff.

130. Or "they."

131. *Mark* 14:14 and *Luke* 22:11 use the same word for "guest room" (*kataluma*).

132. Here the Coptic verb for "hand over" is *paradidou* (from the Greek *paradidonai*), as in the New Testament gospels.

133. Coptic *peuaggelion 'nioudas*, "The Gospel of Judas," "The Gospel About Judas," or "The Gospel for Judas"—not "The Gospel According to Judas."

Chapter Three: Judas in the *Dialogue of the Savior*

1. Nag Hammadi Codex III,5: 120,1–147,23. This translation is based on the Coptic text in Stephen Emmel, ed., *Nag Hammadi Codex III,5* and Pierre Létourneau, ed., *Le Dialogue du Sauveur*. Cf. also Beate Blatz and Einar Thomassen, "The Dialogue of the Savior"; Julian V. Hills, "The Dialogue of the Savior"; Hans-Martin Schenke, Hans-Gebhard Bethge, and Ursula Ulrike Kaiser, eds., *Nag Hammadi Deutsch*, 1.381–97 (Silke Petersen and Hans-Gebhard Bethge). A substantial number of textual restorations have been incorporated here, and many of them have come from these editions, particularly from *Nag Hammadi Deutsch* and also from *Le Dialogue du Sauveur*. More speculative restorations are given in the notes.

2. Lit., "brothers." Here in the *Dialogue of the Savior* the circle of disciples includes Judas (Judas Thomas or Judas Iscariot), Matthew (the disciple Matthew, Matthias the replacement apostle according to *Acts* 1:23–26, or Mathaias the scribe of the *Book of Thomas*), and Mary (probably Mary of Magdala).

3. Or "suffering." Cf. *Gospel of Thomas* 58.

4. Cf. *Gospel of Thomas* 50; 90.

5. Here and below the text reads "it" and the translation follows *Nag Hammadi Deutsch* and reads "anger" for the sake of clarity.

6. Or "solitary." Here and below, cf. *Gospel of Thomas* 16:4; 49:1; 75.

7. Cf. *John* 16:23; *Letter of Peter to Philip* 133–34.

8. Logos.

9. Or "solitary."

10. Cf. *Gospel of Thomas* 3:1–3; 22:4–7; 89.

11. On the phrase "pass by," cf. *Gospel of Thomas* 42.

12. The disciple Matthew, Matthias the replacement apostle according to *Acts* 1:23–26, or Mathaias the scribe of the *Book of Thomas*.

13. Judas Thomas or Judas Iscariot. Cf. the *Gospel of Thomas* and the *Gospel of Judas*.

14. Or "Lord," here and below.

15. Or "[your nature]," "[your belief]."

16. Cf. *Gospel of Thomas* 24.

17. Cf. *John* 16:5–7.

18. Probably Mary of Magdala.

19. Or restore to read "[the strength]." On the fruits of the spirit, cf. *Galatians* 5:22–23.

20. It is also possible to restore this sentence without the negative, but cf. a few lines below, and *Dialogue of the Savior* 133.

21. Here Petersen and Bethge, in *Nag Hammadi Deutsch*, 1.389, restore to read, "[If you resemble] one [who never existed]."

22. Cf. *Genesis* 1:1.

23. Cf. *Genesis* 1:2.

24. Lit., "from [it]."

25. Here Petersen and Bethge, in *Nag Hammadi Deutsch*, 1.390, restore to read "[wickedness thus has no existence]."

26. Or "[Judas] said [to him]."

27. Or "[movement]," "[mind]."

28. Here and below Petersen and Bethge, in *Nag Hammadi Deutsch*, 1.390, restore to read "circumcision."

29. Here and below the restoration is tentative. If the saying discusses physical circumcision and spiritual circumcision, then cf. *Gospel of Thomas* 53; *Romans* 2:25–29.

30. Perhaps read "[are circumcised]."

31. Cf. *Gospel of Thomas* 81:2.

32. Cf. *Gospel of Thomas* 2.

33. Logos, here and below. The text reflects upon the primal water of creation and the place of the word in the creative process, according to *Genesis* 1. Apparently the water is both below and above, as in much of ancient cosmological thought.

34. Or "He"—i.e., the word—here and below.

35. These are the constellations and stars that rule over what happens on the earth, according to astronomical and astrological theory.

36. The restoration is tentative. This may simply be a continuation of the discussion in the previous section.

37. Or "cast," "emit."

38. Or "cast," "emitted."

39. Probably the sun.

40. I.e., the dome of the sky, around the earth, on which the sun, moon, and stars are set. Cf. *Genesis* 1:6–8.

41. Or "worshiped."

42. Or "Son of Man," here and below.

43. Cf. *Gospel of Thomas* 3:5.

44. Cf. the Delphic maxim "Know yourself," and *Gospel of Thomas* 3:4–5.

45. Lit., "it." This refers to the place of life under discussion in the context.

46. Lit., "his goodness" or "its goodness"—the goodness of that person or the goodness of that place.

47. It is also possible to translate this sentence as follows: "The word established the world, and the world came to be through the word, and the world received fragrance from the word." The Coptic text employs ambiguous pronouns throughout the sentence.

48. Lit., "root."

49. On the wind blowing, cf. spirit. On the entire passage, cf. *Genesis* 1:2.

50. Logos. On the role of the word or logos, and Jesus as the incarnate word, cf. *John* 1, earlier passages in the *Dialogue of the Savior*, and other Gnostic texts. In the *Gospel of John*, as here, the word descends from the realm above, comes to this world below, and acts in a revelatory manner.

51. These references to seed, power, and deficiency are typical in Gnostic texts.

52. On garments clothing the soul and on putting on perfect humanity as a garment, cf. *Gospel of Mary* 15; 18. On garments of light and life given to those who enter the bridal chamber, cf. *Dialogue of the Savior* 138–39.

53. For similarly mystical statements, cf. *Gospel of Thomas* 77; 108.

54. The region of deficiency is this world below, where the light is obscured in darkness.

55. Archons, here and below.

56. On the rulers or archons who govern this world, cf. *1 Corinthians* 6:3. On the bridal chamber, cf. the *Gospel of Philip; Gospel of Thomas* 75.

57. On the garments of the soul and the garments of light and life, cf. *Dialogue of the Savior* 136–37; *Gospel of Mary* 15; 18.

58. Cf. *Dialogue of the Savior* 145.

59. Cf. *Matthew* 6:34.

60. Cf. *Matthew* 10:10 (Q); *Luke* 10:7 (Q); *1 Timothy* 5:18.

61. Cf. *Matthew* 10:25. If this third saying is emended by adding a negation ("Disciples do <not> resemble their teachers"; cf. Petersen and Bethge, in *Nag Hammadi Deutsch*, 1.394), then cf. *John* 13:16. Here in the *Dialogue of the Savior* it is Mary who utters these three sayings of wisdom.

62. Or "She spoke this utterance as a woman who understood completely."

63. Cf. *1 Corinthians* 2:9; *Gospel of Thomas* 17; *Gospel of Judas* 47.

64. Cf. *Dialogue of the Savior* 144–45; *Gospel of the Egyptians*.

65. This place is the present world of deficiency and mortality.

66. Going to one's rest at once means dying now, so that this may be a question about why we do not experience the transformation from death to life now, or even why we do not commit suicide now.

67. Leaving the burden of the body behind and ascending to the fullness of the divine means attaining final rest.

68. Cf. *James* 5:3.

69. Cf. *John* 14:5.

70. Here Petersen and Bethge, in *Nag Hammadi Deutsch*, 1.395, restore to read "you [will sustain] everything."

71. The archons and other powers of the cosmos.

72. On putting on the garment of the body and taking it off, cf. *Dialogue of the Savior* 136–39; *Gospel of Mary* 15; *Gospel of Thomas* 21:2–4; 37:2–3.

73. Possibly restore to read "Judas" (Petersen and Bethge, in *Nag Hammadi Deutsch*, 1.395).

74. The restoration is tentative; cf. Petersen and Bethge, in *Nag Hammadi Deutsch*, 1.395.

75. Cf. the parable of the mustard seed in *Gospel of Thomas* 20; *Matthew* 13:31–32 (Q); *Luke* 13:18–19 (Q); *Mark* 4:30–32.

76. Or "Mother of the universe."

77. Or "speaks and acts." Here the Father is God the Father, and the Mother may be Sophia (Wisdom) or another female manifestation of the divine.

78. Or "womanhood," here and below.

79. This statement seems to deny the possibility of being born again.

80. Cf. *Dialogue of the Savior* 140; *Gospel of the Egyptians*; *Gospel of Thomas* 114.

81. Coptic *šaje*; cf. logos.

82. Cf. *Dialogue of the Savior* 135.

83. Cf. *Dialogue of the Savior* 139.

84. About twelve lines missing or untranslatable.

85. The concluding restorations are tentative.

Chapter Four: The Follower Without a Name in the
Concept of Our Great Power

1. Nag Hammadi Codex VI,4: 36,1–48,15. This translation is based on the Coptic text in Pierre Chérix, ed., *Le Concept de notre grande puissance* and Douglas M. Parrott, ed., *Nag Hammadi Codices V,2–5 and VI*, 291–323 (Frederik Wisse and Francis E. Williams). Cf. also Hans-Martin Schenke, Hans-Gebhard Bethge, and Ursula Ulrike Kaiser, eds., *Nag Hammadi Deutsch*, 2.483–93 (Hans-Martin Schenke); Francis E. Williams, *Mental Perception*. The text is also provided with the titles *Intellectual Perception* and the *Concept of the Great Power* (which may be emended; see the note) at the opening of the text.

2. Perhaps emend to read "<Our>," as in the version of the title at the end of the text and the opening line of the text itself.

3. The great Power designates the divine in a number of traditions, including that of Simon Magus. Cf. *Acts* 8:10; *Thunder* 21.

4. When the first person singular pronoun ("I") is used, the speaker often seems to be the great Power.

5. On one hundred twenty years, cf. *Genesis* 6:3.

6. Cf. *Gospel of Thomas* 4.

7. Or "writings." On the letters of God written in the living book, cf. *Gospel of Truth* 22–23.

8. Cf. *Genesis* 1:1–7.

9. Or "he," here and below.

10. Darkness.

11. On creation in the image of God, cf. *Genesis* 1:26; *Secret Book of John* II, 14–15.

12. On the giants and long periods of time, cf. *Genesis* 5:1–6:8.

13. The father of the flesh is the God of this world.

14. Cf. *Genesis* 6:9–9:29.

15. I.e., the flood.

16. The food and water may designate eucharist and baptism.

17. Coptic, from Greek, *nianhomoion* (in Greek *anomoios* means "unlike"). Here some scholars prefer to read "the Anomoeans," and they refer to the mid-fourth century Anomoean heresy, an extreme form of Arian thought that maintained God the Father and Christ were essentially unlike each other. Cf. Wisse and Williams, in *Nag Hammadi Codices V,2–5 and VI*, 304.

18. Coptic *mane;* cf. Greek *mania*. The meaning of the Coptic word is unclear; it could mean "shepherd," but that seems inappropriate in the current context, and *mania* seems more likely. On fire that destroys dwellings and more, cf. apocalyptic fire, and perhaps even the fire that destroyed Sodom and Gomorrah.

19. Cf. Irenaeus of Lyon *Against Heresies* 1.7.1, where Irenaeus reports that in the system of the Valentinian teacher Ptolemy it is said that at the end, when the fire in the world has consumed matter, it will pass into nonexistence.

20. This human is the Gnostic revealer, who comes to expression in the figure of Jesus.

21. Or "in" (Coptic *'n*).

22. Seventy or seventy-two is the traditional number of nations in the world according to Jewish lore. Hence the revealer here is said to speak all the languages of the world.

23. Hades.

24. Cf. *Hebrews* 2:14.

25. Judas Iscariot.

26. Cf. *Gospel of Judas* 56.

27. Coptic *paradidou* (from the Greek *paradidonai*), as in the New Testament gospels and the *Gospel of Judas*.

28. Coptic *paradidou*, once again.

29. This refers to the crucifixion of Jesus.

30. Coptic *berôth*. Some scholars have translated this as "nine bronze coins" (*berôt th*); cf. the payment made to Judas Iscariot according to *Matthew* 26:15; 27:3; Wisse and Williams, in *Nag Hammadi Codices V,2–5 and VI*, 308–9.

31. Cf. *Three Forms of First Thought* 43.

32. Logos, here and below.

33. Cf. *Romans* 10:4; *Ephesians* 2:15.

34. Cf. *Matthew* 27:45; *Mark* 15:33; *Luke* 23:44–45.

35. These comments describe the expansion of the emerging orthodox church and the proclamation of words of Jesus or the composition of texts about Jesus.

36. On one hundred twenty years, cf. *Concept of Our Great Power* 38.

37. Wisse and Williams note, in *Nag Hammadi Codices V,2–5 and VI*, 312, that Philo of Alexandria considers one hundred twenty to be the "perfect number" because it is an "image and imitation of the circle of the zodiac" (*On Rewards and Punishments* [*De praemiis et poenis*] 65).

38. Logos.

39. The east, where the Logos first appeared, is probably Palestine.

40. These images and those that follow are typical of apocalyptic literature.

41. On birds eating the dead, cf. *Ezekiel* 39:17–20; *Revelation* 19:21; Homer, *Iliad* 1.4–5.

42. The paragraphs that follow seem to reflect statements about the activity of the Antichrist as that is described in such texts as Hippolytus of Rome, *On the Antichrist.* Apparently it is thought that the Antichrist will come from the west, imitate the person of Jesus, and attempt to establish Jewish customs.

43. Or "true Sophia."

44. Or "false Sophia."

45. Or "imposter"; Coptic, from Greek *pantimeimon.* Cf. *Revelation of Peter* 71; 78–79.

46. Apparently Jesus the revealer.

47. On this statement and what follows, cf. *Revelation* 13, on the two beasts, those who worship the beasts, and signs and wonders.

48. Apparently the Antichrist.

49. I.e., the cycle of the origin, flow, and replenishment of water in the world will no longer work.

50. Cf. *Excerpt from the Perfect Discourse* 73.

51. In Manichaean sources 1468 years is the period of time of the final conflagration in which the cosmos will burn and the last light particles will be freed from matter and return to paradise. Cf. Schenke, in *Nag Hammadi Deutsch*, 2.492.

52. Cf. Irenaeus of Lyon *Against Heresies* 1.7.1.

53. Coptic *hap*, which could also be translated "judgment."

54. Or "it."

55. Or "its," here and below.

56. Cf. *Secret Book of John* II, 26–27; *Paraphrase of Shem* 48; *Luke* 16:22–24.

57. The final state of those who follow the great Power will be rest in the eternal realm.

Chapter Five: The Traitor in the "Round Dance of the Cross"

1. *Acts of John* 94–96. This translation is based on the Greek text in Eric Junod and Jean-Daniel Kaestli, *Acta Iohannis*. Cf. also Barbara E. Bowe, "Dancing into the Divine"; Arthur J. Dewey, "The Hymn in the Acts of John"; André-Jean Festugière, *Les Actes apocryphes de Jean et de Thomas*, 199–207; Marvin Meyer, "The Round Dance of the Cross"; Knut Schäferdiek, "The Acts of John," 181–84.

2. The devil. In Gnostic texts the creator of this world—i.e., the God of the Jewish people—may be compared to the devil.

3. Cf. the New Testament accounts of Jesus being handed over by Judas. The Greek word used here is *paradothênai* (from *paradidonai*).

4. Logos, here and below.

5. Cf. *1 John* 1:5.

6. Here and below the English translation employs the emphatic future "I will" for the Greek *thelô*, lit., "It is my will to . . ."

7. Instructions for liturgical dance.

8. This may refer to the realm of eight (Ogdoad) in Valentinian thought, i.e., the seven planetary spheres plus the eighth sphere (of the stars). Sometimes the eighth sphere is considered the abode of the ruler of the cosmos; sometimes it is thought to be a higher level for spiritual advancement. Cf. *Secret Book of John*; *Discourse on the Eighth and Ninth*.

9. Cf. the twelve signs of the zodiac.

10. Cf. *John* 10:9.

11. Cf. *John* 14:6.

12. Cf. *Gospel of Thomas* 42.

13. Probably Judas.

14. Cf. Jesus laughing in the *Gospel of Judas*.

15. Or "put to shame."

16. Perhaps cf. *Second Discourse of Great Seth* 55–56; *Revelation of Peter* 81–83.

Chapter Six: Judas the Diabolical in Other Christian Texts

1. Abdullah Yusuf Ali, trans., *The Meaning of the Holy Qur'ân*, 235–36.

2. This translation is based on the Latin text in Constantin von Tischendorf, ed., *Evangelia Apocrypha*, 199–200.

3. James and Joses (or Joseph) are younger brothers of Jesus, along with Judas and Simon, according to *Mark* 6:3 and *Matthew* 13:55.

4. Cf. *John* 19:34. In the *Gospel of John*, one of the Roman soldiers pierces Jesus's side with a spear; in the *Arabic Infancy Gospel*, it is said that the Jews pierce his side.

5. This translation is based on the Greek text in Bart D. Ehrman, ed., *The Apostolic Fathers*, 2.104–7.

6. On this account of Judas's cursed state, cf. *Numbers* 5:21–22.

7. This translation is based on the Greek text in Constantin von Tischendorf, ed., *Evangelia Apocrypha*, 459–64.

8. Gestas is a traditional name of one of the thieves crucified with Jesus.

9. Demas is also a traditional name of one of the thieves crucified with Jesus.

10. Cf. *Tobit* 1–2.

11. A drachma was a Greek silver coin; sources suggest a sheep might be worth one drachma, an ox five drachmai, a slave four drachmai.

12. Tuesday.

13. Cf. *Mark* 14:58; *Matthew* 26:61; *Mark* 15:29; *Matthew* 27:40; *John* 2:19.

14. Wednesday.

15. 3:00 p.m.

16. Or "synagogue."

17. Thursday.

18. Silver coins, here and below?

19. 10:00 a.m.

20. 11:00 a.m.

21. Thursday night.

22. Cf. *Psalm* 1:1 (Septuagint).

23. This translation, prepared by Patrick McBrine, is based on the Latin text in Johann Huemer, ed., *Sedulii Opera Omnia*. Cf. Carl P. E. Springer, *The Gospel as Epic in Late Antiquity*; also the poem, composed by the fourth-century Christian poet Juvencus, entitled *Books of the Gospels*, or *Evangeliorum Libri*.

24. Cf. *John* 13:1–20.

25. Cf. *Matthew* 23:27.

26. Cf. *Zechariah* 11:12–13; *Matthew* 26:15; 27:3, 9–10.

27. This translation is based on the Coptic text in Eugène Revillout, "Les apocryphes coptes," 156–57, 195–96.

28. Cf. *John* 12:6.

29. Cf. *Zechariah* 11:12–13; *Matthew* 27:9–10.

30. This translation is based on the Greek text in Constantin von Tischendorf, ed., *Evangelia Apocrypha*, 290.

31. Cf. *Mark* 14:72; *Matthew* 26:74–75; *Luke* 22:60–62; *John* 18:27 (all regarding Peter and his denial).

32. This translation is based on the Coptic text (of Codex Borgiani Coptici 109, fasc. 132) in X. Jacques, "Les deux fragments conserves des 'Actes d'André et de Paul,'" 198–205.

33. Cf. 2 *Corinthians* 12:1–10; the Nag Hammadi *Revelation of Paul.*

34. Perhaps cf. "the son of perdition" in *John* 17:12.

35. Cf. *Matthew* 18:21–22; also see *Luke* 17:3–4.

36. Cf. *Isaiah* 45:5–6, 21; 46:9. This statement of the singularity of God in the Jewish Scriptures becomes the arrogant boast of the demiurge in Gnostic texts.

37. Michael is one of the archangels in Jewish and Christian lore.

38. This translation is based on the Italian text in Lonsdale and Laura Ragg, eds., *The Gospel of Barnabas,* 470–73, 478–81.

39. Cf. the transformation of Simon of Cyrene to look like Jesus (and Jesus to look like Simon) according to Basilides, as reported by Irenaeus (*Against Heresies* 1.24.4).

40. Cf. *Mark* 14:51–52.

41. Cf. *Psalm* 22:1; *Mark* 15:34; *Matthew* 27:46 (in the New Testament texts Jesus is the one who cites *Psalm* 22:1).

42. This translation is based on the Coptic text in E. A. Wallis Budge, ed., *Coptic Apocrypha in the Dialect of Upper Egypt,* 6–9.

43. The children of Abraham.

44. About three or four lines missing.

45. Cf. *Acts* 1:20; *Psalm* 109:8 (108:8, Septuagint). The Coptic word used in the *Book of the Resurrection of Christ* for "position as overseer" (or "office of bishop") is m'ntepiskopos.

46. According to the text, Judas is filled with the vices enumerated.

47. About eight lines partially missing. In these lines mention is made of the Jews, and it is said that Judas is cast into outer darkness and forgotten forever.

48. This translation, prepared by Jonathan Meyer, is based on the Latin text in Giovanni Paolo Maggioni, ed., *Iacopo da Varazze: Legenda Aurea,* 2.277–81. Cf. also Granger Ryan and Helmut Ripperger, eds., *The Golden Legend of Jacobus de Voragine.*

49. Cf. *John* 6:71; 13:2, 26. For Ruben, cf. the name Reuben.

50. On this story of Judas and his father and mother, cf. Sophocles, *Oedipus Rex.*

51. Cf. *John* 12:1–8. On three hundred denarii, cf. *John* 12:5.

52. Cf. *Matthew* 27:5.

53. Cf. *Acts* 1:18.

54. Cf. *Acts* 1:13–26.

Chapter Seven: Traitors Before Judas

1. This translation is based on the Hebrew text of the Jewish Scriptures.

2. In the Greek of the Septuagint, Judas.

3. His brothers.

4. Cf. thirty pieces of silver or thirty silver coins in accounts of Judas handing over Jesus, especially *Matthew* 26:15; 27:3, 9, with the notes.

5. Lit., "to Sheol."

6. This translation is based on the Hebrew text of the Jewish Scriptures.

7. Cf. *John* 13:18.

8. This translation, prepared by Jonathan Meyer, is based on the Greek text of Homer.

9. Eumaeus.

10. Telemachus.

11. Perhaps cf. the New Testament accounts of Judas, one of the Twelve, coming to Jesus with an armed contingent.

12. Perhaps cf. the account of Judas being hanged in *Matthew* 27:3–10.

13. Perhaps cf. the account of the horrible death of Judas in *Acts* 1:13–26.

SELECTED BIBLIOGRAPHY

Aland, Kurt, ed. *Synopsis Quattuor Evangeliorum: Locis parallelis evangeliorum apocryphorum et partum adhibitis.* 15th rev. ed. Stuttgart: Deutsche Bibelgesellschaft, 1996.

Anderson, Ray S. *The Gospel According to Judas.* Colorado Springs: Helmers & Howard, 1991.

Barnstone, Willis, and Marvin Meyer, eds. *The Gnostic Bible.* Boston: Shambhala, 2003.

Bauer, Walter. *Orthodoxy and Heresy in Earliest Christianity.* Philadelphia: Fortress, 1971.

Bianchi, Ugo, ed. *Le Origini Dello Gnosticismo: Colloquia di Messina, 13–18 Aprile 1966.* Studies in the History of Religions (Supplements to *Numen*) 12. Leiden: Brill, 1970.

Blatz, Beate, and Einar Thomassen. "The Dialogue of the Savior." In *New Testament Apocrypha*, edited by Wilhelm Schneemelcher, 1.300–312.

Borges, Jorge Luis. "Three Versions of Judas." In *Labyrinths.* New York: New Directions, 1964.

Bowe, Barbara E. "Dancing into the Divine: The Hymn of the Dance in the *Acts of John.*" *Journal of Early Christian Studies* 7 (1999): 83–104.

Brown, Raymond E. *The Death of the Messiah.* 2 vols. Garden City, NY: Doubleday, 1994.

Budge, E. A. Wallis, ed. *Coptic Apocrypha in the Dialect of Upper Egypt.* London: British Museum, 1913.

Chérix, Pierre, ed. *Le Concept de notre grande puissance (CG VI,4): Texte, remarques philologiques, traducion et notes.* Orbis Biblicus et Orientalis 47. Fribourg and Göttingen: Vandenhoeck & Ruprecht, 1982.

Crossan, John Dominic. *Who Killed Jesus? Exposing the Roots of Anti-Semitism in the Gospel Story of the Death of Jesus.* San Francisco: HarperSanFrancisco, 1995.

Culianu, Ioan. "The Gnostic Revenge: Gnosticism and Romantic Literature." In *Religionstheorie und Politische Theologie, Band 2: Gnosis und Politik*, edited by Jacob

Taubes, 290–306. Munich, Paderborn, Vienna, and Zurich: Wilhelm Fink/ Ferdinand Schöningh, 1984.

———. *The Tree of Gnosis: Gnostic Mythology from Early Christianity to Modern Nihilism*. Translated by H. S. Wiesner. San Francisco: HarperSanFrancisco, 1992.

de Boer, Esther A. "Mary Magdalene and the Disciple Jesus Loved." *Lectio Difficilior* 1 (2000): electronic journal (http://www.lectio.unibe.ch).

DeConick, April D. *The Thirteenth Apostle: What the Gosepl of Judas Really Says*. New York and London: Continuum, 2007.

Dewey, Arthur J. "The Hymn in the Acts of John." *Semeia* 38 (1986): 67–80.

Doresse, Jean. *The Secret Books of the Egyptian Gnostics: An Introduction to the Gnostic Coptic Manuscripts Discovered at Chenoboskion*. Translated by Philip Mairet. London: Hollis & Carter, 1960.

Ehrman, Bart D. *The Lost Gospel of Judas Iscariot*. New York and Oxford: Oxford University Press, 2006.

———, ed. *The Apostolic Fathers*. Loeb Classical Library. 2 vols. Cambridge, MA: Harvard University Press, 2003.

Emmel, Stephen, ed. *Nag Hammadi Codex III,5: The Dialogue of the Savior*. Nag Hammadi Studies 26. Leiden: Brill, 1984.

The Facsimile Edition of the Nag Hammadi Codices. Published under the auspices of the Department of Antiquities of the Arab Republic of Egypt in conjunction with the United Nations Educational, Scientific and Cultural Organization. 12 vols. Leiden: Brill, 1972–84.

Fallon, Francis T. *The Enthronement of Sabaoth: Jewish Elements in Gnostic Creation Myths*. Nag Hammadi Studies 10. Leiden: Brill, 1978.

Festugière, André-Jean, ed. *Les Actes apocryphes de Jean et de Thomas*. Cahiers d'orientalisme 6. Geneva: P. Cramer, 1983.

Foerster, Werner, ed. *Gnosis: A Selection of Texts*. Translated by R. McL. Wilson. 2 vols. Oxford: Clarendon, 1974.

Gärtner, Bertil E. *Iscariot*. Translated by Victor I. Gruhn. Philadelphia: Fortress, 1971.

Grant, Robert M. *Gnosticism and Early Christianity*. New York: Columbia University Press, 1966.

Grant, Robert M., ed. *Gnosticism: An Anthology*. New York: Harper, 1961.

Haardt, Robert, ed. *Gnosis: Character and Testimony*. Leiden: Brill, 1971.

Haenchen, Ernst. *The Acts of the Apostles: A Commentary*. Translated by Bernard Noble, Gerald Shinn, Hugh Anderson, and R. McL. Wilson. Philadelphia: Westminster, 1971.

Halas, Roman Bernard. *Judas Iscariot: A Scriptural and Theological Study of His Person, His Deeds and His Eternal Lot.* Studies in Sacred Theology 96. Washington, DC: Catholic University Press, 1946.

Halm, Heinz. *Die islamische Gnosis: Die extreme Schia und die 'Alawiten.* Die Bibliothek des Morgenlandes. Zurich: Artemis, 1982.

Hedrick, Charles W., and Robert Hodgson, Jr., eds. *Nag Hammadi, Gnosticism, and Early Christianity.* Peabody, MA: Hendrickson, 1986.

Hills, Julian V. "The Dialogue of the Savior." In *The Complete Gospels: Annotated Scholars Version,* edited by Robert J. Miller, 336–50. Santa Rosa, CA: Polebridge, 1994.

Huemer, Johann, ed. *Sedulii Opera Omnia.* Corpus Scriptorum Ecclesiasticorum Latinorum 10. Vienna: C. Geroldi, 1885.

Jacques, X. "Les deux fragments conserves des 'Actes d'André et de Paul.'" *Orientalia* 38 (1969): 187–213.

Jonas, Hans. *Gnosis und spätantiker Geist.* Part 1. Forschungen zur Religion und Literatur des Alten und Neuen Testaments 51. Göttingen: Vandenhoeck & Ruprecht, 1964.

———. *The Gnostic Religion: The Message of the Alien God and the Beginnings of Christianity.* Boston: Beacon, 1963.

Junod, Eric, and Jean-Daniel Kaestli, eds. *Acta Iohannis.* Corpus Christianorum, Series Apocryphorum 1–2. Turnhout: Brepols, 1983.

Kasser, Rodolphe, Marvin Meyer, Gregor Wurst, and François Gaudard, eds. *The Gospel of Judas, Together with the Letter of Peter to Philip, James, and a Book of Allogenes, from Codex Tchacos.* Washington, DC: National Geographic, 2007.

Kasser, Rodolphe, Marvin Meyer, and Gregor Wurst, eds. *The Gospel of Judas.* Washington, DC: National Geographic, 2006.

Kazantzakis, Nikos. *The Last Temptation of Christ.* Translated by P. A. Bien. New York: Simon & Schuster, 1960.

Kemner, Heinrich. *Judas Iskariot: Zwischen Nachfolge und Verrat.* Stuttgart: Neuhausen, 1988.

King, Karen L. *What Is Gnosticism?* Cambridge, MA: Harvard University Press/ Belknap Press, 2003.

Klassen, William. *Judas: Betrayer or Friend of Jesus?* Minneapolis: Fortress, 1996.

———. "Judas Iscariot." In *The Anchor Bible Dictionary,* edited by David Noel Freedman, 3.1091–96. New York: Doubleday, 1992.

Klauck, Hans-Josef. *Judas—Ein Jünger des Herrn.* Quaestiones Disputatae 111. Freiburg: Herder, 1987.

Kloppenborg, John S. *Q Parallels: Synopsis, Critical Notes and Concordance.* Sonoma, CA: Polebridge, 1988.

Kloppenborg, John S., Marvin W. Meyer, Stephen J. Patterson, and Michael G. Steinhauser. *Q—Thomas Reader.* Sonoma, CA: Polebridge, 1990.

Koester, Helmut. *Ancient Christian Gospels: Their History and Development.* Philadelphia: Trinity; London: SCM, 1990.

Koester, Helmut, and Elaine H. Pagels. "Introduction." In *Nag Hammadi Codex III,5: The Dialogue of the Savior,* edited by Stephen Emmel, 1–17.

Koester, Helmut, Elaine H. Pagels, and Stephen Emmel. "The Dialogue of the Savior." In *The Nag Hammadi Library in English,* edited by James M. Robinson, 244–55.

Krosney, Herbert. *The Lost Gospel: The Quest for the Gospel of Judas Iscariot.* Washington, DC: National Geographic, 2006.

Layton, Bentley. *The Gnostic Scriptures: A New Translation with Annotations and Introductions.* Garden City, NY: Doubleday, 1987.

———. "Prolegomena to the Study of Ancient Gnosticism." In *The Social World of the First Christians: Essays in Honor of Wayne A. Meeks,* edited by L. Michael White and O. Larry Yarbrough, 334–50. Minneapolis: Fortress, 1995.

———, ed. *The Rediscovery of Gnosticism: Proceedings of the International Conference on Gnosticism at Yale, New Haven, Connecticut, March 28–31, 1978.* Studies in the History of Religions (Supplements to Numen) 41. Leiden: Brill, 1980–81.

Létourneau, Pierre, ed. *Le Dialogue du Sauveur.* Bibliothèque copte de Nag Hammadi, Section "Textes" 29. Québec: Les Presses de l'Université Laval; Louvain: Peeters, 2003.

Lüdemann, Gerd, and Martina Janssen. *Bibel der Haretiker: Die gnostischen Schriften aus Nag Hammadi.* Stuttgart: Radius, 1997.

Maccoby, Hyam. *Judas Iscariot and the Myth of Jewish Evil.* New York: Free Press, 1992.

MacDonald, Dennis R. *Does the New Testament Imitate Homer? Four Cases from the Acts of the Apostles.* New Haven, CT: Yale University Press, 2003.

———. *The Homeric Epics and the Gospel of Mark.* New Haven, CT: Yale University Press, 2000.

———. *Mimesis and Intertextuality in Antiquity and Christianity.* Studies in Antiquity and Christianity. Harrisburg, PA: Trinity Press International, 2001.

Mack, Burton L. *The Lost Gospel: The Book of Q and Christian Origins.* San Francisco: HarperSanFrancisco, 1993.

Maggioni, Giovanni Paolo, ed. *Iacopo da Varazze: Legenda Aurea.* 2 vols. Florence: Sismel, 1998.

Mahé, Jean-Pierre, ed. *Hermès en Haute Égypte (Tome I): Les textes hermétiques de Nag Hammadi et leurs parallèles grecs et latins.* Bibliothèque copte de Nag Hammadi, Section "Textes" 3. Québec: Les Presses de l'Université Laval; Louvain: Peeters, 1978.

———. *Hermès en Haute Égypte (Tome II): Le Fragment du Discours Parfait et les Définitions hermétiques arméniennes.* Bibliothèque copte de Nag Hammadi, Section "Textes" 7. Québec: Les Presses de l'Université Laval; Louvain: Peeters, 1982.

Mahé, Jean-Pierre, and Paul-Hubert Poirier, eds. *Écrits gnostiques.* Bibliothèque de la Pléiade. Paris: Gallimard, forthcoming.

Marjanen, Antti, ed. *Was There a Gnostic Religion?* Publications of the Finnish Exegetical Society 87. Helsinki: Finnish Exegetical Society; Göttingen: Vandenhoeck & Ruprecht, 2005.

Markschies, Christoph. *Valentinus Gnosticus? Untersuchungen zur valentinianischen Gnosis mit einem Kommentar zu den Fragmenten Valentins.* Tübingen: J. C. B. Mohr (Paul Siebeck), 1992.

Meyer, Marvin. *The Gnostic Discoveries: The Impact of the Nag Hammadi Library.* San Francisco: HarperSanFrancisco, 2005.

———. *The Gnostic Gospels of Jesus: The Definitive Collection of Gnostic Gospels and Mystical Books About Jesus of Nazareth.* San Francisco: HarperSanFrancisco, 2005.

———. *The Gospel of Thomas: The Hidden Sayings of Jesus.* San Francisco: HarperSanFrancisco, 1992.

———. "The Round Dance of the Cross." In *The Gnostic Bible,* edited by Willis Barnstone and Marvin Meyer, 351–55.

———, ed. *The Nag Hammadi Scriptures: The International Edition.* San Francisco: HarperOne, 2007.

Miller, Robert J., ed. *The Complete Gospels: Annotated Scholars Version.* Santa Rosa, CA: Polebridge, 1994.

Muhammad Ali, Maulana, trans. *The Holy Qur'ân: Arabic Text, English Translation and Commentary.* Columbus, OH: Ahmadiyyah Anjuman Isha'at Islam, 1994.

Orbe, Antonio. *Estudios Valentinianos.* Analecta Gregoriana 99. Rome: Pontificia Università Gregoriana, 1958.

Paffenroth, Kim. *Judas: Images of the Lost Disciple.* Louisville, KY: Westminster/John Knox, 2002.

Pagels, Elaine H. *Beyond Belief: The Secret Gospel of Thomas.* New York: Random House, 2003.

———. *The Gnostic Gospels.* New York: Random House, 1979.

Pagels, Elaine H., and Karen L. King. *Reading Judas: The Gospel of Judas and the Shaping of Christianity.* New York: Viking, 2007.

Parrinder, Geoffrey. *Jesus in the Qur'an.* New York: Oxford University Press, 1965.

Parrott, Douglas M, ed. *Nag Hammadi Codices V, 2–5 and VI with Papyrus Berolinensis 8502,1 and 4.* Nag Hammadi Studies 11. Leiden: Brill, 1979.

Patterson, Stephen J., James M. Robinson, and Hans-Gebhard Bethge. *The Fifth Gospel: The Gospel of Thomas Comes of Age.* Harrisburg, PA: Trinity Press International, 1998.

Pearson, Birger A. *Gnosticism and Christianity in Roman and Coptic Egypt.* Studies in Antiquity and Christianity. New York and London: T. & T. Clark International, 2004.

————. *Gnosticism, Judaism, and Egyptian Christianity.* Studies in Antiquity and Christianity. Minneapolis: Fortress, 1990.

————. "Judas Iscariot and the *Gospel of Judas.*" Institute for Antiquity and Christianity Occasional Paper 51. Claremont, CA: Institute for Antiquity and Christianity, 2007.

Perkins, Pheme. *Gnosticism and the New Testament.* Minneapolis: Fortress, 1993.

Petersen, Silke, and Hans-Gebhard Bethge. "Der Dialog des Erlösers." In *Nag Hammadi Deutsch,* edited by Hans-Martin Schenke, Hans-Gebhard Bethge, and Ursula Ulrike Kaiser, 1.381–97.

Ragg, Lonsdale and Laura, eds. *The Gospel of Barnabas.* Oxford: Clarendon, 1907.

Ragg, Lonsdale and Laura, eds., with commentary by M. A. Yusseff. *The Gospel of Barnabas.* New Delhi: Millat Book Centre, n.d.

Revillout, Eugène. "Les apocryphes coptes: I. Les Évangiles des douze apôtres et de Saint Barthélemy." In *Patrologia Orientalis* 2.2, edited by René Graffin, 117–98. Paris: Firmin-Didot, 1904, reprinted 1946.

Robinson, James M. "From the Cliff to Cairo: The Story of the Discoverers and Middlemen of the Nag Hammadi Codices." In *Colloque international sur les texts de Nag Hammadi (Québec, 22–25 août 1978),* edited by Bernard Barc, 21–58. Bibliothèque copte de Nag Hammadi, Section "Études" 1. Québec: Les Presses de l'Université Laval, 1981.

————. "Nag Hammadi: The First Fifty Years." In Stephen J. Patterson, James M. Robinson, and Hans-Gebhard Bethge, *The Fifth Gospel,* 77–110.

————. *The Secrets of Judas: The Story of the Misunderstood Disciple and His Lost Gospel.* San Francisco: HarperSanFrancisco, 2006.

————, ed. *The Nag Hammadi Library in English.* San Francisco: HarperSanFrancisco, 1988.

Robinson, James M., Paul Hoffman, and John S. Kloppenborg, eds. *The Critical Edition of Q: Synopsis Including the Gospels of Matthew and Luke, Mark, and Thomas with English, German, and French Translations of Q and Thomas.* Louvain: Peeters, 2000.

Rudolph, Kurt. *Gnosis: The Nature and History of Gnosticism*. English translation edited by R. McL. Wilson. San Francisco: HarperSanFrancisco, 1987.

Ryan, Granger, and Helmut Ripperger, eds. *The Golden Legend of Jacobus de Voragine*. New York: Longmans, Green, 1941.

Sagnard, François. *La gnose valentinienne et le témoignage de Saint Irénée*. Paris: Vrin, 1947.

Schäferdiek, Knut. "The Acts of John." In *New Testament Apocrypha*, edited by Wilhelm Schneemelcher, 2.152–212.

Schenke, Hans-Martin. "Das sethianische System nach Nag-Hammadi-Handschriften." In *Studia Coptica*, edited by Peter Nagel, 165–72. Berlin: Akademie, 1974.

Schenke, Hans-Martin, Hans-Gebhard Bethge, and Ursula Ulrike Kaiser, eds. *Nag Hammadi Deutsch*. 2 vols. Die Griechischen Christlichen Schriftsteller der ersten Jahrhunderte, Neue Folge, 8, 12. Berlin and New York: Walter de Gruyter, 2001, 2003.

Schneemelcher, Wilhelm, ed. *New Testament Apocrypha*. English translation edited by R. McL. Wilson. 2 vols. Cambridge: James Clarke; Louisville, KY: Westminster/John Knox, 1991–92.

Scholem, Gershom G. *Jewish Gnosticism, Merkabah Mysticism, and Talmudic Tradition*. New York: Jewish Theological Seminary of America, 1960.

———. *Kabbalah*. New York: Plume, 1978.

———. *Major Trends in Jewish Mysticism*. New York: Schocken, 1995.

———. *On the Kabbalah and Its Symbolism*. New York: Schocken, 1996.

———. *Origins of the Kabbalah*. Princeton, NJ: Princeton University Press, 1991.

Scholer, David M. *Nag Hammadi Bibliography 1948–1969*. Nag Hammadi Studies 1. Leiden: Brill, 1971.

———. *Nag Hammadi Bibliography 1970–1994*. Nag Hammadi Studies 32. Leiden: Brill, 1997.

Schwager, Raymund. *Must There Be Scapegoats? Violence and Redemption in the Bible*. Translated by Maria L. Assad. San Francisco: Harper & Row, 1987.

Schwarz, Günter. *Jesus und Judas: Aramaistische Untersuchungen zur Jesus-Judas Überlieferung der Evangelien und der Apostelgeschichte*. Beiträge zur Wissenschaft vom Alten und Neuen Testament 123. Stuttgart: Kohlhammer, 1988.

Scopello, Madeleine, ed. *L'Évangile de Judas: Le contexte historique et littéraire d'un nouvel apocryphe*. Colloque international tenu à Paris, Université de Paris IV-Sorbonne les 27–28 octobre 2006. Nag Hammadi and Manichaean Studies. Leiden: Brill, forthcoming.

Sevrin, Jean-Marie. *Le dossier baptismal séthien: Études sur la sacramentaire gnostique*. Bibliothèque copte de Nag Hammadi, Section "Études" 2. Québec: Les Presses de l'Université Laval, 1986.

Sieber, John H. "The Barbelo Aeon as Sophia in Zostrianos and Related Tractates." In *The Rediscovery of Gnosticism*, edited by Bentley Layton, 788–95.

Smith, Jonathan Z. *Drudgery Divine: On the Comparison of Early Christianities and the Religions of Late Antiquity.* Chicago: University of Chicago Press, 1990.

Spong, John Shelby. *Liberating the Gospels: Reading the Gospels with Jewish Eyes.* San Francisco: HarperSanFrancisco, 1996.

Springer, Carl P. E. *The Gospel as Epic in Late Antiquity: The Paschale Carmen of Sedulius.* Supplements to *Vigiliae Christianae* 2. Leiden: Brill, 1988.

Stead, G. C. "The Valentinian Myth of Sophia." *Journal of Theological Studies* 20 (1969): 75–104.

Stroumsa, Gedaliahu A. G. *Another Seed: Studies in Gnostic Mythology.* Leiden: Brill, 1984.

Tardieu, Michel. *Écrits gnostiques: Codex de Berlin.* Sources gnostiques et manichéennes 1. Paris: Cerf, 1984.

Tischendorf, Constantin von. *Evangelia Apocrypha.* Lipsiae: H. Mendelssohn, 1876.

Turner, John D. "Sethian Gnosticism: A Literary History." In *Nag Hammadi, Gnosticism, and Early Christianity,* edited by Charles W. Hedrick and Robert Hodgson, Jr., 55–86.

Turner, John D. *Sethian Gnosticism and the Platonic Tradition.* Bibliothèque copte de Nag Hammadi, Section "Études" 6. Québec: Presses de l'Université Laval; Louvain: Peeters, 2001.

van der Vliet, Jacques. "Judas and the Stars: Philological Notes on the Newly Published Gospel of Judas (*GosJud,* Codex Gnosticus Maghâgha 3)." *The Journal of Juristic Papyrology* 36 (2006): 137–52.

Vermes, Geza. *Jesus the Jew.* Philadelphia: Fortress, 1973.

Vogler, Werner. *Judas Iskarioth: Untersuchungen zu Tradition und Redaktion von Texten des Neuen Testaments und außerkanonischer Schriften.* Theologische Arbeiten 42. Berlin: Evangelischer Verlag, 1983; 2d. ed., 1985.

Wagner, Harald, ed. *Judas Iskariot: Menschliches oder Heilsgeschichtliches Drama?* Frankfurt: Knecht, 1985.

Williams, Francis E. *Mental Perception: A Commentary on NHC VI,4, The Concept of Our Great Power.* Nag Hammadi and Manichaean Studies 51. Leiden: Brill, 2001.

Williams, Michael A. *The Immovable Race: A Gnostic Designation and the Theme of Stability in Late Antiquity.* Nag Hammadi Studies 29. Leiden: Brill, 1985.

——. *Rethinking "Gnosticism": An Argument for Dismantling a Dubious Category.* Princeton, NJ: Princeton University Press, 1996.

Wright, N. T. *Judas and the Gospel of Jesus: Have We Missed the Truth About Christianity?* Grand Rapids, MI: Baker, 2006.

Yusuf Ali, Abdullah, trans. *The Meaning of the Holy Qur'ân.* Beltsville, MD: Amana, 1999.

ACKNOWLEDGMENTS

I wish to express my thanks to Chapman University and the Griset Chair in Bible and Christian Studies for the support of my research on this book. For my work on the *Gospel of Judas*, the National Geographic Society has been generous in providing access to the Codex Tchacos, and the collaborative work on the *Gospel of Judas* with Rodolphe Kasser and Gregor Wurst, along with François Gaudard, forms the foundation for the translation and notes published here. Several people at HarperOne have been particularly helpful in guiding this book through the intricacies of the publishing process, and among them I acknowledge Eric Brandt, Kris Ashley, Ralph Fowler, and Lisa Zuniga. I offer special thanks to Patrick McBrine and Jonathan Meyer for their translationsof important selections providing insights into traditions about Judas Iscariot.